2

Cajun Sketches

From the Prairies of Southwest Louisiana

/Cajun Sketches/

From the Prairies of Southwest Louisiana

BY LAUREN C. POST

LOUISIANA STATE UNIVERSITY PRESS
BATON ROUGE AND LONDON

P.B. 134

Copyright © 1962 by Louisiana State University Press
Manufactured in the United States of America
All rights reserved

Louisiana Paperback Edition, 1990
99 98 97 96 95 94 93 92 91 90   5 4 3 2 1

Library of Congress Cataloging-in-Publication Data
Post, Lauren C.
    Cajun sketches, from the prairies of southwest Louisiana / by
Lauren C. Post.—Louisiana paperback ed.
    p.   cm.
    Includes bibliographical references.
    ISBN 0-8071-1605-X
    1. Cajuns.   2. Louisiana—Social life and customs.   I. Title.
F380.A2P67   1990
976.3'5004410763—dc20   90-31294
                                               CIP

Contents

Illustrations

Preface

I was born in Acadia
Parish in southwest Louisiana, but I can scarcely qualify as a Cajun
because my father and mother were of Anglo-Saxon stock from
Mississippi and New York, respectively. While quite young, I became fairly proficient in speaking Cajun French. This fortunate
accomplishment helped me to acquire an appreciation of the old
Acadian ways and to write a dissertation in geography at the University of California on "The Cultural Geography of the Prairies
of Southwest Louisiana."

This volume is a modification of the dissertation with more
stress on Acadian life and with less of the discipline that ordinarily
goes with dissertations.

Whenever full names, such as Aldus Broussard, the late Sidney
Broussard, or Edna Mae Arceneaux, are used, they refer to very
real people. Where only the given names, such as Emile, Basil, or

Baptiste are used, there is no intent to make reference to any particular individual. The happenings, however, are very true to Acadian life.

For information and assistance I am grateful to dozens of residents of the Cajun country. Many of them were interviewed during the 1930's, and where ages are given below, the figures indicate ages at the time of interview. Of course some information comes from my own memories which go back into the first decade of this century. Listed below are some of the more important informants. They are not in order of importance.

C. J. Arceneaux, teacher and agricultural agent, Duson and Thibodaux
Edna Mae Arceneaux, pupil, Rayne
the late Sidney Arceneaux, operator of a *boucherie de campagne* near Bosco
Warren Arceneaux, farmer near Rayne
Adolphina Benoit, weaver from near Carencro
Octave Bertrand, aged eighty, farmer near Faquetaïque
the late George K. Bradford, aged eighty-one, a surveyor of much of southwest Louisiana
Aldus Broussard, fiddler from Rayne
Mrs. Marie Campbell, aged ninety-three, resident of Lafayette
the late Gradney Cochran, cattle brand recorder from Lafayette
Mrs. Vertalee Comeaux, housewife from Lafayette
"La Vieille Arçin Cook," deceased, Choctaw woman from Bayou Queue de Tortue
Joseph Falcon, accordion player and singer from Rayne and Crowley
Wilfred Falcon, farmer near Duson
the late Robert Hoffpauir, miller and carpenter from Duson and Rayne
the late Oneziphore Guidry, operator of a *fais-dodo* near Rayne
Henry Lastrapes, clerk of St. Landry Parish
the late Jake Lockley, chairmaker from Rayne
Gaston Moore, syrup maker from Plaquemine Brulée
Joseph Moore, house mover from Mermentau
Celin Prejean, aged eighty, millwright from St. Pierre
André Olivier, store keeper and historian from St. Martinville

Jack Preston, aged eighty-one, Negro steamboat man from the town of
  Washington
the late John (Beebee) Richard, aged sixty-six, Negro from Duson and
  Rayne
the late Popon Senegal, Negro from Duson and Rayne
Elmore Sonnier, singer from Scott and Mobile (Alabama)
the late Cleobule Thibodeaux, farmer from Duson
Evelyn Broussard Walker, singer from Lake Arthur and Jennings
Lawrence Walker, accordion player and singer from Rayne
the late Blanchard K. Whitfield, early settler and photographer from Duson and Lafayette
Irene Thérèse Whitfield, long-time observer of Acadian ways, from Duson and Lafayette

For many intimate details, I am grateful to my deceased father
and mother, Mr. and Mrs. William Whitfield Post, for their keen
observations and dependable memories. My brothers Harry and
Melvin, both of whom had very close relations with the Acadians,
likewise have been of invaluable assistance.

Among the professors who have helped through their direction
are Fred B. Kniffen, Richard J. Russell, J. B. Francioni, and Henry
V. Howe of Louisiana State University; T. Lynn Smith of the
University of Florida; and John B. Leighly and Carl Sauer of the
University of California.

LAUREN C. POST

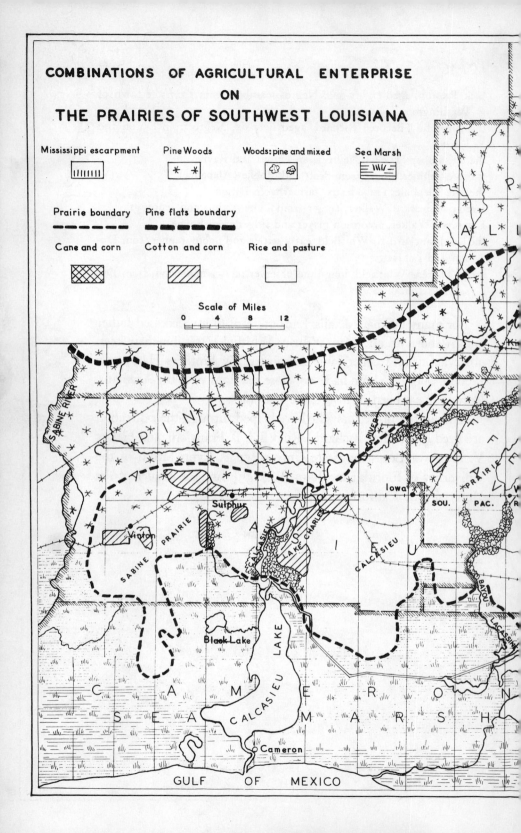

COMBINATIONS OF AGRICULTURAL ENTERPRISE
ON
THE PRAIRIES OF SOUTHWEST LOUISIANA

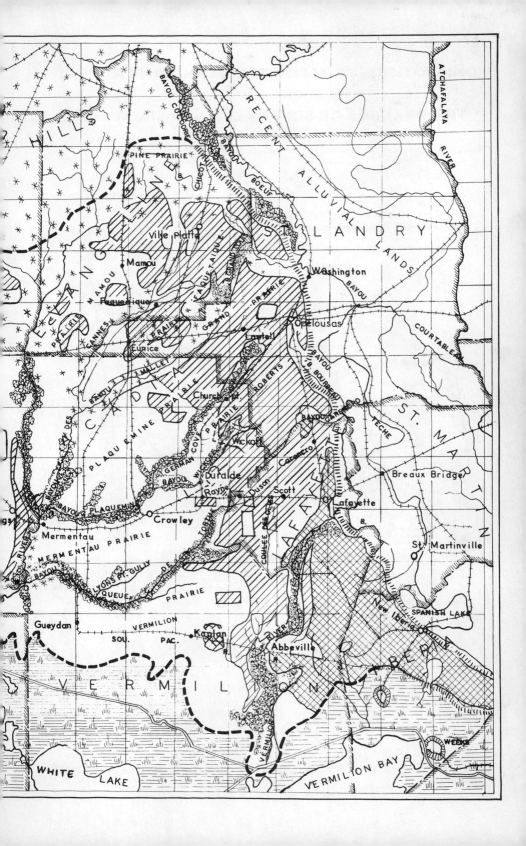

1

The Exiles

AND talk about Cajuns!
Why, down in their country I knew two families that had eighteen
children apiece, and no one thought anything of it. There were
lots of big families in those days—so many that the five thousand
or so original Acadians who came to Louisiana showed a hundred-
fold increase and now number about half a million.

Fictionalized though they were through Longfellow's poem
Evangeline, the Acadians are very real and form an important
group of people in Louisiana. The poem gave the American public a sketch of their coming, and American histories and writings
have added to general knowledge of them, but the real story of
Cajun country is not generally known outside the state of Louisiana. In fact, many of the Acadians themselves do not know
the significance of their own ways and how they created a chapter
in American cultural history that is different from all others in
the state and country.

Their expulsion from Nova Scotia took place in 1755. Ten years later many of the exiles who had wandered about in the eastern seaboard colonies and even in the West Indies began to arrive at New Orleans and other places along the Mississippi River.

"Free at last and under the flag of France"—but there was another surprise in store for them. Louisiana had been transferred to Spain, and now they were in Spanish, not French, territory. They also found that they were not wanted in or even near New Orleans. Some were sent to the "Acadian Coasts" on the banks of the river above the city, some to Bayou Lafourche, and others to the country of the Attakapas and Opelousas Indians. That was in the southwest part of the present Louisiana where there were two insignificant little Spanish posts called the Poste des Attakapas at the present site of St. Martinville and the Poste des Opelousas where the town of Opelousas now stands. The former is on the famous Bayou Têche; the latter near Bayou Courtableau at the prairie's eastern edge. In those days, by the water routes traveled and in the rowboats or *bateaux* used by the people, it probably took them nearly a month to make the journey from the Mississippi to Attakapas.

Although many of these people arrived in Louisiana eleven years before the signing of the Declaration of Independence, others of them trickled in years later, and some who had gone back to France arrived as late as 1785. A few of the latter intermarried with the French people, but soon they were so intermixed that little distinction was made between those who had been back to France and those who had not. With the Louisiana Purchase in 1803, they all became American citizens regardless of who they were or where they had been born.

It will be noted that throughout this book the writer uses the words Acadian and Cajun interchangeably. They mean the same thing, merely, people of Acadia. And the Acadia referred to is the old French Acadia or *Acadie,* now called Nova Scotia. When one is speaking formally, one says Acadian. When one is speaking informally, one says Cajun. Thus Cajun is a corruption of Acadian. In similar manner, *Cajin* is a corruption of *Acadien*. The shifting from one term to the other merely expresses a degree of formality or degree of corruption of speech.

It should never be implied that Cajun and Negro are in any way related. Cajuns are white people, and although there has been racial mixing, the people resulting from the mixing are referred to as Negroes or as colored people.

The word Creole means something entirely different. It really means "produced in the colonies" or simply "home grown." Creoles were born in the colonies of European ancestry. There were French, Spanish, and Portuguese Creoles, as well as Creoles of many other origins. Formerly, Negroes born in the colonies were referred to as Creole Negroes as contrasted with imported slaves. The latter were called *bosals* because they were supposed to be wild, and it was necessary to put halters on them. In time, the white people dropped these appellations, and it came to be that in cities such as New Orleans, being a Creole was tantamount to belonging to the elite class, whether of French or Spanish descent.

As examples of how the word Creole is used to mean "home grown," note these illustrations. Locally produced butter and eggs are Creole products; those from outside the local area are referred to as American products. The old French newspapers of Louisiana advertised for sale "American horses" and "Creole horses." People spoke of "American mules" and "Creole mules." The former were from Missouri and Tennessee, the latter were the home-grown kind. Creole chairs were the homemade chairs. Those people who have visited in south Louisiana will recall having been asked whether they wanted northern coffee or Creole coffee.

In Nova Scotia the Acadians had been mainly farmers and fishermen. They excelled in the reclaiming of tidal flats for farming by building dykes, and they had been considered quite successful in their stock raising and general subsistence farming. And today it is still the *petit paysan* or *habitant* who is most characteristically "Acadian" and who is perhaps least subject to change. This type seems to have best preserved the old Acadian customs.

The refugee Acadians had to start at the bottom of the economic scale, for they were poverty stricken. They were sent to lands that were subject to frequent overflow and which were occupied mainly by Indians. On the prairies they became stock-raisers. They registered their cattle brands at St. Martinville, and annually they rounded up their stock and branded their calves after the manner of the Spanish-American cattle raisers in other parts of Latin America. Many elements of this pastoral economy undoubtedly were borrowed from the Spanish under whose domination the Acadians lived for more than a third of a century. Yet, as will be pointed out later, the Acadians never became as proficient cowhands as the vaqueros of Texas, New Mexico, or California. The prairies were especially suited to the raising of half-wild cattle, and on them the Acadians established their ranches or *vacheries*. The cattle were sold in New Orleans and to the planters along the Mississippi. This distinctive industry continued on the prairies until the last of them was plowed up, and even today, in modified form, the industry persists in the coastal marshes. It is significant that for more than a century and a quarter, cattle raising was the main industry of the prairie Acadians, and it dominated their lives during most of that time.

In portions of the prairies some Acadians later engaged in raising rice wher that industry came into prominence, and probably these Acadians diverged farther from the original Acadian culture than did the sugar and cotton planters. Certainly they have shown greater enterprise than the Acadian cotton farmers.

Some who remained on the Têche also turned to farming—the raising of sugar cane, cotton, and corn. In those lands, sugar became the main agricultural product, and many Acadians, along with other planters, engaged in its production. Sugar planters were often large landholders, and they rose to greater prominence than the *petit paysan,* or small farmer, who engaged in the raising of cotton and corn. The Acadians have also contributed heavily to the fisherfolk, trappers, and moss gatherers of Louisiana. The commercial fishermen along the coast and in the bayous, the boatmen, the muskrat trappers, and the moss gatherers show a great deal of the Acadian heritage. However, the Acadians of this book are predominantly prairie dwellers. Many of them have never seen a pirogue.

One of the most distinctive features of Acadian culture is the Louisiana-French language, the only language which many of them speak even today. Their reticent nature and physical isolation militate against their learning English and, in turn, their linguistic isolation made it possible for them to maintain many of their own ways in but slightly changed form. Without the advantage of the public school, they seldom learned to read and write, and because they spoke only French, they were able to maintain more of their own customs without making the changes through which most other groups of Americans have passed. Language was probably the common denominator of the Acadian heritage, but even the language varies from section to section.

Since the public schools have been made accessible to all children of Louisiana, and attendance has been made compulsory, all Acadian children are now learning to speak, read, and write in English. There can be no more generations of Louisianians who cannot speak our language, and the Acadians will become more and more like other Americans.

Many Acadians have been Americanized, but, in turn, many Americans have been Gallicized by them. In dozens of towns and communities in south Louisiana the Acadian dialect is the main language spoken. In the courthouses located in Ville Platte, Opelousas, Crowley, Lafayette, Abbeville, St. Martinville, and New Iberia, it is not at all uncommon to find groups of men conversing over legal matters, the weather, and the local happenings, all in the Acadian dialect except for the modern words which they sprinkle in along with the French.

The events and episodes of this book take one from the early settlements through the height of the *vacherie* period to the present period of rather intensive agricultural development and the trend toward modernization. The economic transition is nearly complete, but not so the folkways of the Acadian people, for they change more slowly than did their economy. Each locale offers its own story against its own background, and invariably there is something in the story that does not belong to the great American melting pot. These people are conspicuously rural; their religion is without exception Roman Catholic; the older ones seldom read or write any language; they have strong family ties; and there is considerable homogeneity in their culture over large areas. However, their uniqueness lies in their French-Acadian dialect and the strong development of a great maze of folkways in which they live and carry on their economy.

These sketches and tales from Cajun country were recorded especially for the purpose of shedding light upon the disappearing culture of the old pastoral Acadians (especially as represented in Lafayette and Acadia parishes) who later took up the raising of cotton and corn on the old Attakapas Prairie. These people received their education, not with the help of the printed page, but rather by the events which seemed so fundamental to them and those which served to break the monotony of what might otherwise have been a very humdrum existence. Happenings in all stages of life, from the cradle to the grave show the uniqueness of these people—for example, their courtship and marriage; their novel methods of farming and animal husbandry; their music, singing, and dancing.

The material for this work was collected in many ways and from many different sources, but most of it was obtained from actual contact with the people and from first-hand observations. "Old timers," once started on their numerous recollections, contributed a fair share.

Cajun country has always been rich in material for geographers, historians, sociologists, anthropologists, linguists, and creative artists. Each had a vast fund of information to offer, and each helped to enrich the reader's conception of Cajun country. The writer believes that the reading of this book will give a true picture of the past lives of the Acadians and certainly the culture herein described has applied to many now living. Much of it can be observed at the present time.

The writer feels indebted to the Acadians for many of his most pleasant recollections from the state of Louisiana. No one could work among them without learning to appreciate their ways of living or without feeling that their ways are not inferior to others. Perhaps we should feel sorry that many of these pleasant and genuine old folkways are passing out, for the Acadians are truly a most charitable and hospitable people.

Early Approaches
to the Acadian Prairies

T HE earliest approaches to Southwest Louisiana from the city of New Orleans were by intricate systems of navigation following rivers and bayous, sometimes going upstream, and sometimes down, but nevertheless by water throughout. The most important route went by way of Bayou Plaquemine, a distributary of the Mississippi, which leaves the river 132 miles above New Orleans and branches off in such a manner as to reach the Atchafalaya River, from whence boats could readily ascend Bayou Têche to the sites of St. Martinville and Breaux Bridge. Another route made use of Bayou Lafourche, likewise a distributary of the Mississippi which leaves it at the present town of Donaldsonville. It was thus that entry was made into the Attakapas country in seasons of high water.

The route to the Opelousas country was along the Courtableau, a large bayou which also flows into the Atchafalaya River. It is formed by the joining of the Boeuf and Cocodrie above the present town of Washington, the town which became the head of navigation for the boats which came from the Mississippi.

The above routes were followed during the high-water stages, which lasted through a good part of the year. During very low water there was no flow from the Mississippi into its distributaries. Then boats had to ascend the Mississippi to the junction of the Red River, pass through the Old River, and from it descend into the Atchafalaya, a very circuitous route. Down that river they came, and those bound for the Opelousas and Boeuf countries entered the Courtableau, while those carrying Attakapas traffic descended to the mouth of the Têche and then ascended that stream to their desired destinations.

It was over these complex bayou routes that boats reached the Attakapas and Opelousas areas from about 1765 until the Southern Pacific Railroad was built about 1880. Now one travels the route from Plaquemine or Baton Rouge to Opelousas in about sixty minutes on a modern highway, quite a contrast to the difficulties of bayou travel of the old days. Early writers left detailed descriptions of their voyages to the countries of Attakapas and Opelousas. Following is a schedule of distances in miles from Plaquemine to St. Martinville, as given by William Darby in 1818 in his *Emigrant's Guide to the Western and Southwestern States and Territories:*

NEW ORLEANS TO NEW IBERIA AND ST. MARTINVILLE
BY PLAQUEMINE, ATCHAFALAYA AND TECHE RIVERS

Mouth of Plaquemine	132
Bayou into Lake Natchez	142
Lake Natchez	144
Re-enter Atchafalaya	154
Mouth of Têche	175
Renthrop's	180
Outlet of Lake Chitimachas	191
Courthouse of St. Mary's	206
Smith's	219

In 1805 Thomas C. Nichols, son of the *Grand Juge* of the County of Attakapas, made the trip to his new station and wrote about it in his "Reminiscences," the original of which is in the possession of his granddaughter, Mrs. Mary Flower Pugh Russell. The account tells of about a week's travel from New Orleans to Plaquemine by "hack," a portage made in an oxcart to a landing on Bayou Plaquemine, and the hiring of a boat which was to take the passengers to the Têche. The story even tells of boatmen eating the passengers' supply of provisions in addition to those allowed them for the trip. The boats moored at night but few slept. If the mosquitoes and the alligators did not keep the passengers awake, the carousals of the boatmen did. The labyrinthine network of streams and bayous presented such a perplexity of appearance that the passengers felt lost throughout all of the middle part of the course. To them, all of the streams looked alike, and they felt themselves at the mercy of an undependable crew.

The packet of the Ohio and Mississippi soon invaded the Têche country, and such steamboats later replaced the *bateaux,* with their crews of oarsmen. The first *paquebot,* or steam packet, reached St. Martinville in 1826. *The Planters' Banner,* an exceedingly interesting old newspaper published in Franklin, described some of the early packets, especially the *Banner of Attakapas.* She was "hewn out of our Attakapas forests" and was one hundred and fifty feet long, forty-three feet wide, and when light, she drew only twenty-two inches of water. Seaworthiness was not a requisite in this service, but rather the opposite characteristic was desired. Shallowness of draft was important, especially when a packet had to be dragged over a bar by using a capstan to wind in a rope that was tied to a tree on the bank ahead. Another newspaper, *The Attakapas Gazette* of St. Martinville, carried advertisements in 1841 for a number of boats. Among them were the *Bayou Belle,* the *Ajax,* the *Zephyr,* the *Fusilier,* and the *A. Porter.* In 1859 *Le Courier du Têche,* published in St. Martinville, advertised regular trips of a "packet des Attakapas" called *La Belle Créole,* J. Richardson, "Capitaine."

In spite of the great distances and the inconveniences of travel, the Attakapas country managed to share some of the modern luxuries, as revealed by one writer in *The Planters' Banner* in 1847. Describing James Porter's plantation on the Têche, he wrote: "I find that even here ice is regularly brought by the steamboat from New Orleans, a distance of nearly 300 miles by the route taken. Thus the Yankees, by their accustomed shrewdness, are indirectly driving a brisk trade in exchanging the congelations of the wintery north for the crystallizations of the sunny south."

Until the removal of the Great Raft on the Red River, water from that stream spilled over into bayous such as the Cocodrie, Boeuf, and others, until finally water from the Red entered the Têche. The Boeuf and Cocodrie then generously supplied the Courtableau with water throughout most, if not all, of the year. Washington was then a thriving port on the Courtableau, and it remained so until the removal of the Red River Raft indirectly caused it to decline. As one sees the old landing site today, one wonders how it could ever have been such a thriving port. With its decline, Opelousas took advantage of the change and became the inland town with railroad connections. It grew at the expense of Washington. An interesting chapter on transportation to the prairies closed with the *bateau-à-vapeur,* or steamboat.

The Southern Pacific Railroad and Highway 90 now run parallel to each other across the prairies in an east-west direction and are extremely important lines of land travel. The railroad has been important since the eighties, but the highway, before World War I was a deplorable country dirt road, graveled in the twenties; it was later paved to make a modern thoroughfare.

3

The Natural Setting

THE Attakapas and Opelousas Indians gave their names to two areas, both of which become basic to the old Cajun prairie country. In the former area, Poste des Attakapas was established on Bayou Têche at the present site of St. Martinville. In the latter, Poste des Opelousas was established about six miles from Bayou Courtableau at the present site of Opelousas. From about 1763 each of those focal points served its respective territory in keeping up communications with the older settlements on the Mississippi River. Immediately west of the two posts lay about four thousand square miles of natural grasslands which the French-speaking people called *prairies*.

Those people had a way of applying interesting names to places and things, and in southwest Louisiana their talent was not wasted. The streams, as elsewhere, they called *bayous*. Each individual grassland was called a prairie, and specific names were

4

given to about twenty of them. To the north of the prairies were *les pinières,* or piney woods. To the south, along the Gulf Coast, lay the marshes, in which there were old barrier beaches. To those old oak ridges they gave the name *chenières.* On the prairies, any old abandoned drainage channel was called a *coulée,* and a small circular pond, of which there were thousands on the prairies, they called a *platin.*

A regional map of Louisiana shows that the main prairie region is shaped like a leg of mutton with the big end toward the east near St. Martinville and Opelousas, and the small or shank end at the west near the Sabine River. The slope of the region shows a slight but important drop toward the southwest, thus giving a southwesterly trend to the dozen or more bayous and rivers which drain the area. Since strips of woods parallel the banks of most of the bayous for much of their courses, the woods likewise show a northeast-southwest trend or orientation. Each separate grass-land or prairie was given a name, and each woodland normally took the name of the bayou along which it was situated. Thus, there was a Plaquemine Prairie, a Plaquemine Brulée Bayou, and a Plaquemine Woods, all bordering on each other.

Early writers described the prairies as being grass covered and slightly rolling so as to remind them of the sea. The woods, with their projections and irregularities here and there, reminded them of a shore with points. Church Point and Long Point probably derived their names from such features. Some of the smaller prairies they called coves, and and Prairie Robert, pronounced with a strong French accent, later was called Robert's Cove. Later on, when oak groves grew up around farm houses, they were called islands. As an example, Navarre's grove was called Isle Navarre. Although the individual prairie names are little used today, early maps and writings showed them to be quite important.

In 1873 Colonel Samuel H. Lockett wrote about his trip across the prairies on horseback, guided by his compass. In his manuscript "Louisiana As It Is" he said:

All of this extensive area thus defined as the *Great Prairies* is not one treeless expanse. *Coulees* and *bayous* course through it, generally in a north and south direction, on the borders of which grow fine forests and timber. From the principal belts of timber spurs run into the open prairies like headlands into the sea, thus dividing the whole region into separate tracts each having its own name. Faquetaique, Mamou, Calcasieu, Sabine, Vermilion, Mermentau, Plaquemine, Opelousas, and Grand Prairies are the largest. There are many others with local names that it is needless to mention. The surface of the Prairies, though generally level, is yet not perfect, one cannot ride through the Prairies without having this resemblance to large bodies of water constantly recurring to his mind. The grass that grows upon their surface waves in the wind, and looks like ripples on the bosom of the ocean, the dark blue borders of promontories, the "Coves" like bays and bluffs, and the occasional clumps of trees like islands in the sea.

Morphologically, the prairies can be said to be a portion of an old delta of the Mississippi River, one formed during Pleistocene time. The old river flowed across this region when the land was relatively lower and sea-level actually higher than at present. Old meander scars appear in all aerial photographs taken in the eastern portion of the prairies, although they are scarcely apparent to one traveling on the surface. And to one acquainted with landforms of the Mississippi, its natural levees and meander scars, the story becomes immediately apparent. The natural levees which were built up during overflow of the river in flood stage are always higher near the river and lower in lands which are called the "backlands." Thus the present-day levees of the river have "frontlands" near the river banks which are relatively high, and backlands a couple of miles back which are low and toward which the overflow and seepage waters always go.

It was the relict frontlands of the prairies which attracted early settlers. They were anxious to locate on the high ridges which were a few feet higher than the backlands. On them the soil was deeper and coarser. Altogether, frontlands were much more desirable than the backlands which gathered and held the water. Soils of the east end of the prairies always were more highly regarded than those in the west. The east end had much less of a claypan than the west, and for varied agriculture it was much better. The claypan played an important part in the rice industry which later developed in the western part of the prairies.

The grass which most of the old inhabitants associate with the prairies is not really a native to this country. It is carpetgrass, introduced into the United States from Central America and the West Indies at some time before 1832 and brought into the prairies at some early time. Whatever the native grasses were, many of them were crowded out of vast areas by the carpetgrass, which the Acadians call *gazon*. Although it has been a great competitor against other grasses, it is not especially nourishing for cattle nor can it stand much winter frost. Other more recently introduced grasses in many places are displacing it. The woods contain the usual southern hardwoods such as oak, hickory, gum, magnolia; along the bayous and stream courses there usually are cypress and other water-loving trees.

Conditions on the prairies were favorable for the raising of half-wild cattle. With the heavy rainfall, grass grew well during a long season, but unfortunately it would be killed easily by frost during cold winters. Even during the dry spells there was no water problem for the cattle, as they could drink in the ponds, *coulées,* and bayous. There were no great natural enemies or predatory animals to worry about, so the cattle could usually manage for themselves without any care from their owners except at branding time.

On the negative side it should be stated that the grass was of poor quality as compared with grasses in some of the other sections of the country. There were flies, mosquitoes, and ticks. The latter carried the tick or Texas fever, which for many years made it impossible for southern cattlemen to introduce good stock to improve their herds. Hot weather in summer and cold spells during the more severe winters handicapped the cattle industry. But for the casual cattlemen conditions were satisfactory, and the industry grew.

The Seasons on the Prairies

For a fair description of the old Acadian prairies, one should differentiate and describe all four seasons, for a description of only one season would be most unjust to the other three. Nor should one depend merely upon statistics from the thermometer and the raingauge for descriptive data on the seasons. The seasonal changes in the vegetation and crops, the weather at the different times in the year, and the routines of the farmers and cattlemen are far better indicators of the seasons than are any instruments. The weather elements, in the yearly cycle, make four entirely different landscapes.

Winter

Although the winters are short they bring about a dullness in the landscape thought to be characteristic only of climates of far more northerly latitudes. Few trees on the prairies besides live oaks and pines stay green through the winter months. The deciduous trees, of course, shed their leaves, and the annuals leave no trace of green. Long before Christmas the sugar cane stubble and leaves, the corn stalks, cotton stalks, and the rice stubble have lost all suggestion of the verdant aspect they showed in the spring and summer. The contrast is complete, and the same strong contrast is to be found in the old natural pastures and roadside weeds.

Throughout the winter the local weather conditions are expressed rather well by the wind directions. High pressure to the north sends cold winds unimpeded down the Mississippi Valley, and such winds have been known to force temperatures from the seventies to the lower twenties within a twenty-four-hour period. These cold spells, although of but a few days duration, have been the terror of the prairies. They affect man and beast alike, as neither is prepared for really cold weather. During the great cattle-raising period on the prairies, large numbers of cattle perished during some winters when exposed to the north winds.

The winter of 1877 brought forth news items like the following within twenty or thirty miles of the Gulf: "Cattle are commencing to perish from the inclemency of the weather and lack of forage, and if the winter continues as severe as it is now, the grim skeletons which will dot the surface of the prairies will be legion." C. C. Robin, a Frenchman who traveled in the prairies in the early years of the last century, painted a gruesome picture of the great numbers of cattle lost during some winters from cold and starvation. The same catastrophes have occurred time and again during the present century. These severe losses were due more to lack of feed than to low temperatures, but the lack of forage was in turn due to the cold.

The pastures were ruined by a peculiar condition. Heavy frosts during drought at the beginning of the winter killed the grass; then it was susceptible to decay from the warm rains which followed. Wet rotting ruined the grass. If the rains had preceded the frost, the grass would not have been seriously injured.

While cattle struggled against the cold and starvation, hogs had their most lavish season. They had their low ebb during the summer season when they were confined to small pens. But after All Saints' Day when, according to the custom of the people, all crops had to be in, hogs were turned out to glean the corn fields and potato patches.

Between the cold spells, the balmy winds from the Gulf blow and ultimately bring rain. The winter is thus a succession of changes between cold north winds and warm south winds, the former bringing clear, cool days and the latter warm, mild conditions with considerable precipitation. An intermediate type of condition is clear weather with little wind, during which the daily insolation causes temperatures to rise and brings about the sunny days which attract tourists to the South. It is during those days of the late winter and early spring that the farmers do their early field work.

Spring

With the advance toward spring the fields are plowed, and each additional plowed patch adds to the surface of grays, browns, and blacks until about the first of March, when every square foot of land that is to be planted has been turned. Then vision across the fields is least impaired by vegetation and, seemingly, there are no greens in the landscape except the live oaks, conifers, and some young grass which is just beginning to grow in the pastures.

With the warm days of early spring, budding and growth of leaves bring some of the most abrupt changes of the year, changes that can be exceeded only by a prematurely early frost in the fall. The crops, although planted early, fail for a time to obscure the ground. The flatness of the entire landscape is maintained throughout March. Some corn may be planted in February, but ordinarily March is corn-planting time. Corn and sugar cane are the first crops to manifest themselves, but even their early growth seems slow.

Cotton is planted a little later than corn, and between April tenth and fifteenth, hundreds of farmers are seen putting in their crops. Cotton grows very slowly for a month or so and, of all the plants, native or cultivated, it seems to be most retarded in imposing a verdant aspect upon the landscape.

While cotton planters are busy, rice farmers are also busy making every minute count. Their crop makes a more sudden change in the landscape than does cotton, for as soon as the rice is a few inches high, it is flooded by artificial irrigation. Flooding usually goes on in the month of May, and as the young plants are not entirely submerged, they form a most pleasing mass of green.

As indicated, farm work is carried on during the spring months at full capacity. The different crops dovetail sufficiently in their needs to keep farmers busy, so that it is not until the lay-by which comes in May for the corn and about the end of June for the sugar cane and cotton, that the teams get their hard-earned rest. After that there are only the sweet potatoes to be planted and worked.

Summer

Summer rains are quite unpredictable, as are those of all seasons. Sometimes dry spells last for weeks on end, causing the corn crop to burn, and at other times rain comes in great or small quantities for forty consecutive days. Usually the rains begin to come with considerable regularity about June 8, which is St. Medard's Day. Sensible temperatures are augmented by the very high relative humidity, and the steamy air of some hot, wet days is perhaps the most impressionable feature of the summers of south Louisiana. Although "fanned and tempered by the breezes of the Gulf," it is still too humid for the greatest exertion and comfort.

July usually is a month of rest and relaxation for both man and beast. Odd jobs such as fixing fences and cutting wood occupy a great deal of the time of the more industrious, but little that one can do now will help or hinder the making of the crop. Cultivation of cotton continues later now and the better varieties make it mature earlier, so some farmers "lay down the hoe only to pick up the cotton sack." One should not forget that "on the Fourth of July we most generally have ripe figs, green corn, and watermelons." August then finds cotton picking and rice cutting at their height.

Fall

Corn is gathered immediately after the cotton is picked, but the cutting of cane never begins until after the middle of October. Cane cutting is delayed as long as possible, for the growers know that each additional cool fall day increases the sucrose content of the cane.

Summer and fall hurricanes sometimes visit the prairies and leave in their wakes a number of felled chinaberry trees, but these storms were not feared, and were seldom taken seriously by the inhabitants until Hurricane Audrey struck in 1957.

The leaves of the catalpa trees fall in September. The chinaberry trees keep theirs a little longer, and they turn a beautiful yellow with the first frost, which is apt to come in November. In the rice field, the mass of green turns to a rich yellow and does not lose its beauty even when it is in the shock. The cotton fields whiten as the bolls open, but the pickers soon change the scene to one of stalks with only a few fast-turning leaves upon them. Sugar cane holds its color longest, yielding its green only with the first frost, which turns its leaves to a light buff color. The dangers of frost, rain, and mud are to be avoided, so the planters speed up the work of cutting so as to finish in December, and thus the last of the crops is harvested. The winter draws on, and the cycle is completed.

5

Ponds and Water Supply

FRENCH settlement in Louisiana was for a long time confined to the banks of the rivers and bayous. This was indicated by the riverbank type of land ownership pattern followed by the French and Spanish. Access to water was an important feature of the pattern, whether it was for transportation or for domestic use. The old Acadians kept boats on the streams; they fished in the streams; they watered their stock in them; and they themselves used the water.

As the cattle industry took the settlers away from the woods and into the open prairies of the southwest, they soon found themselves too far away from permanent water supplies. The bayous were in some cases a dozen or more miles apart, so other sources of water were needed. For the cattle, the answer lay in the tens of thousands of little circular ponds which nearly everywhere dotted the prairies. They were in a scattered distribution, and

ACADIAN FARM HOUSE located by a prairie pond. These circular ponds dotting the prairies were used for watering stock and for producing rice in the Oriental method.

fully as often as not, they were on the higher ground. They were merely shallow depressions ten or twelve inches deep, flat bottomed, with steep sides or edges. The smaller ones dried up during any long dry spell, but the larger ones were pretty reliable sources of water for the cattle. Seldom was a pond good for fishing, but any perennial pond was good for crawfish. A frugal Cajun housewife would set out two dozen or so little ducks in a pond in the spring, and for them she collected handsomely in late summer or fall. It was an easy way to raise ducks.

Many of the nicest ponds were located on the higher land of the old corn-and-cotton country of Lafayette and Acadia parishes where the land was homesteaded at a rather early time. House after house had a beautiful pond fifty or sixty yards in diameter near it. Little water entered them from ditches, and usually none left them. Rainfall was their only source of water, and evaporation caused their only losses aside from what the livestock drank.

Horses occasionally wallowed in the ponds, but hogs were usually kept out of the big ones. Of course the people never drank pond water, as cattle milled about in them, especially during fly and mosquito time. It was this milling which undoubtedly made them in the first place. Cattle will stand in any puddle during such times, and they carry considerable amounts of mud on their feet when they leave. Besides that, they cut away the edges of the ponds and thereby cause them to grow in size. It seems that the cutting action of the hooves stopped when the claypan, locally called hardpan, was reached. Some of the old-timers called ponds *des trous de toreau,* or bull holes. This name would indicate that cattle made the ponds themselves, and this explanation seems as logical as any.

Usually a Cajun called a nice, well-shaped pond a *platin;* a poor, irregular one he called a *marais,* or swamp. One particular pond in Acadia Parish was fenced in, back in the eighties, as a sort of Oriental rice patch. Willow fence posts were used, and in a short while they took root and grew into a circle of big trees. These willows made fine shade for the cattle as they stood in the water long after the rice planting was given up. The last of the trees was blown down by a windstorm in 1935.

Water for household use usually came from wells. A man with a large family and with much livestock always dug a well about four or five feet square and about twenty feet deep. This much he lined with bricks or boards. He then bored an additional ten or twenty feet with an augur to insure a good supply of water.

The little farmer or sharecropper merely bored a well with an augur, put in a wooden casing, and, for drawing water, he used a long slender bucket and a rope. When he could afford it, he put in a hand pump.

WATER SUPPLY on the prairie. At many a farmstead or sharecropper's house, a small bored-well furnished water for the house and the livestock.

But the women always wanted soft water for washing. The cistern was the answer for some, but the rain barrel was far more common. For some unknown reason, in the northern part of the prairies, cisterns were usually placed underground. In the southern part they seem to have been placed invariably above ground.

With the passing of time, many of the ponds have been purposely drained or done away with by filling, but many of the nicer ones are still in use. Occasionaly, when an Acadian farmer had no pond for his hogs, he dug a small one. This he called a "dig." "He dug a dig for his hogs."

The windmill has never been very common on the Cajun prairies. Undoubtedly, the little ponds rendered them unnecessary, for it was very common practice for a Cajun to complain of his bad luck when he had to pump water by hand for his cattle.

ACADIAN FARMER standing by his "dig" from which his stock drank. (Photograph taken in 1935.)

6

Early Settlement
and Land Ownership Patterns

P<small>ATTERNS</small> of individual holdings of land have been of interest to geographers and sociologists for many years. Southwest Louisiana is an interesting place for the study of two separate and very distinct such patterns. One is called the "riverbank pattern" and the other the "checkerboard pattern." The former was used to the exclusion of all others by the early French and Spanish for the granting of land in Louisiana, along the rivers and bayous, and it is also quite well known for its extensive use on the St. Lawrence River in Canada, where it was introduced earlier by the French. These holdings usually are long narrow strips, so the system is sometimes referred to as the "strip system." The checkerboard system is the Rectangular System of Surveys which was later introduced by the United States Land Office. It is the commonly known system of survey based upon the use of townships, sections, and quarter sections, in which all holdings seem to be squares or combinations of squares.

A physical feature which greatly favored the riverbank system was the natural levees of both the rivers and the bayous. Usually these levees were higher near the stream course, and they sloped gently toward the backlands. They were built up over ages of time by the flooding of the streams, and for obvious reasons the flooding waters dropped most of their loads, particularly the favored silty materials, near the banks. Hence the preference for the higher and more easily drained lands near the streams.

On a favored river or bayou bank site, a settler could have water, a means of transportation, high ground for his house and field, and still his own land ran back to the woods, so he could have every resource of the area right on his own land. But there was an economic and sociological advantage to be gained by the riverbank system of settlement. Since all settlers built on the banks, they were side by side, and everyone had neighbors. To people of Latin extraction this was an important consideration. To the Scotch-Irish who settled in the woods country, the opposite was the case. They wanted isolation, and under a system of settlement where all land holdings were squares, they usually got it. Today in bayou country, but not in true prairie country, roads still follow the bayous generally, and whoever lives on the bayou or river is within easy access of the mailman, the school bus, the telephone and power lines, and even the gas and water lines.

In the riverbank system of holdings, each grant began at the bank of the stream and extended at a right angle toward the backlands, whether these were swamps, woods, or prairie. Thus each holding along a straight stream was a rectangle, while holdings along curved streams formed triangles or trapezoids, triangles on the inner curve, and trapezoids on the outer. The ordinary depth, or *profondeur ordinaire,* was forty arpents, an arpent being about 193 feet. The width also was expressed in arpents (*arpents de face*), so a tract of six arpents of front and usual depth really measured six by forty arpents. The sale of an arpent of front involved the sale of a tract one arpent (193 feet) by forty arpents—if the tract faced a portion of the river without curves. As subdivision for a long time was almost invariably lengthwise, there are today many long, narrow tracts or holdings along the rivers and bayous of south Louisiana. The same condition arose in French Canada along the St. Lawrence River, where the system has been in operation for more generations.

A unique method of expressing land quality evolved following the spread of the riverbank pattern. On the Têche the highest frontland was designated *terre de la première qualité.* Just back of that land was lower land assessed as *terre de la deuxième qualité.* Beyond that was the *terre de la troisième qualité,* and in places there was a fourth class of land, *terre de la quatrième,* but undoubtedly, that was more water than land. An old slave census from St. Martinville recorded the number of arpents of front of each plantation and also the number of slaves on each plantation for the entire length of Bayou Têche. From the Têche, Courtableau, and Boeuf, the riverbank land pattern spread to the bayous of the prairies proper. Once in use, the type was never changed.

Because all early settlement was along the water courses, the riverbank land pattern is confined to the rivers and bayous. Practically all woodlands of the prairie region fell within this pattern. The open prairies remained unclaimed for a long time, and only after 1803, which was the beginning of the American period, were they settled. Those open spaces were referred to as *au large,* or areas at large.

In the prairies at large, the United States Land Office did the surveying, the mapping, and the apportioning out of the land, usually under the Homestead Act. Thus, a map of Plaquemine Prairie shows the two distinctive patterns, the one in use along the bayous, and the other in use in the open prairie. This pattern, of course, is based upon townships, ranges, sections, and quarter sections. It is as systematic as the pattern which one would see in

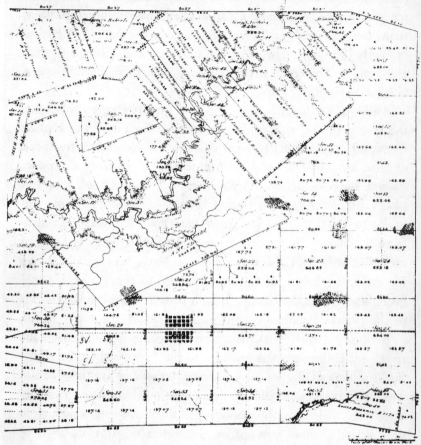

T. 9 S~R. 2 E. *South Western District La.*

PLAT MAP of a characteristic township in Acadia Parish in 1882, showing clearly the riverbank and the rectangular survey types of land ownership patterns. The town shown is Rayne, which is located on the
Southern Pacific Railroad.

flying over Kansas or Iowa. The two patterns join with a very
irregular boundary line, one which at times causes the roads to
shift courses in passing from one system to the other. In places
main roads parallel the bayous, but there are many exceptions. In

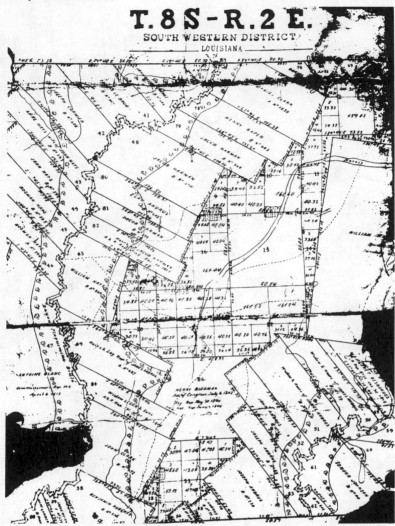

PART OF AN OLD PLAT MAP showing land grants on Bayou Plaquemine
Brulée and some of the prairie at large which was homesteaded in the
pattern of the United States Land Office Survey.

the checkerboard pattern, one might expect to find a road along
each section line.

The towns and villages are laid out on rectangular patterns
as elsewhere in the United States. The older foundings usually are

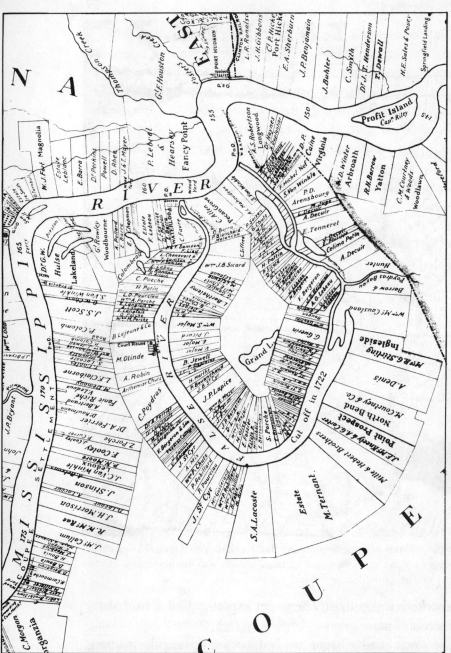

THE RIVERBANK PATTERN of land ownership illustrated by a map from Point Coupee and a section of the Mississippi River. The area shown is not in southwest Louisiana, but it illustrates the pattern followed in all of south Louisiana. (This map was copied from Persac's Map Showing Plantations along the lower Mississippi River, 1858.)

on stream courses and were affected by the riverbank land pattern in their orientations. Those founded on open prairies, especially after the United States Land Office survey, usually have north-south and east-west streets in true checkerboard fashion.

Acadian farmers plow their fields in rows that go up and down the old riverbank pattern of ownership, following a pattern established on the prairies during the Spanish occupation. Once this pattern is set, nothing but the most drastic of economic changes could prevent it from being recognizable a thousand years hence.

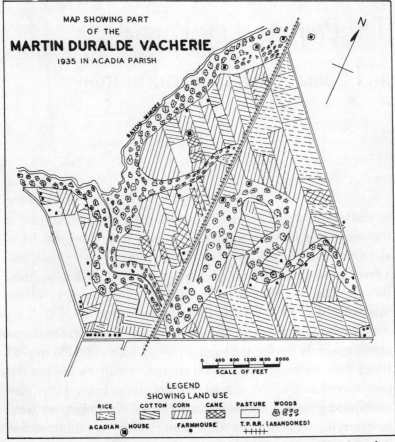

LAND USE MAP for 1935. The orientation of field patterns remains after nearly two centuries.

7

The Peopling of the Prairies and Some Acadian Acculturation

Four great waves and several minor waves of immigration brought the greater part of the population into the prairies. Of course there were Attakapas and Opelousas Indians, and there were some French people and a few Spaniards in the area before the coming of the Acadians. But the Acadians formed the first of the great waves following their expulsion by the British from Nova Scotia in 1755. They came to the old Poste des Attakapas and to the Poste des Opelousas, arriving mainly during the twenty-year period from 1765 to 1785. From these starting places, which are not actually on the prairies, they moved first to the eastern parts of the prairies, where they multiplied greatly. Some settled in the area to the immediate west; however, the western parts of the prairies were very thinly settled. The fecundity of this group was of greatest importance in the peopling of the prairies, and their natural increase in numbers from a well unified group can scarcely be overestimated in its importance in establishing a homogeneous culture on the prairies.

The second movement was that of Americans of Anglo-Saxon origin into the Opelousas area beginning about the time of the Revolutionary War and continuing well into the middle of the last century. Theirs was a segment of a great movement of Americans westward through the southern states, due in part to exhaustion of the more eastern lands and the consequent seeking of new lands to the west. Old records in the St. Landry Parish courthouse at Opelousas are replete with names of settlers belonging to this group, and the several Opelousas newspapers give plenty of evidence of the settlement in the area of many English-speaking settlers from other parts of the country.

The Negro slaves made a third group. Large numbers of them were brought to Attakapas and Opelousas from the southeastern states as well as from other sections of Louisiana. As Negroes make up about half of the population of some sections, they naturally outnumbered any particular white group. They assumed the cultures, and particularly the languages, of their white neighbors, whether the latter spoke English or French. They were originally far more important to the sugar cane planters to the east of the prairies than they were to the cattle-raising Acadians, but after the Civil War they penetrated all parts of the prairies.

Another group of some importance resulted from the mixing of white people, particularly the French-speaking, with Negroes. The resultant mixing or crossing produced a group of peculiar social position called *Gens Libres de Couleur,* or Free People of Color. Their existence in southwest Louisiana, as well as in other parts of the state, has long been known, but the "Brand Book for the District of Opelousas and Attakapas, 1760-1888" showed in an impressive way that there were great numbers of these free people of mixed blood before the Civil War.[1] In every way they placed

[1]Dr. E. D. Johnson, Director of the Stephens Memorial Library, University of Southwestern Louisiana, made it possible for the writer to obtain a microfilm copy of the entire brand book. This and other courtesies are gratefully acknowledged here.

themselves much higher than their Negro slave neighbors. So prominent and wealthy were some of them that they could and did own Negro slaves. Since many of them owned cattle brands, they must have had cattle, and many of them also owned land.

The Free People of Color in the Cane River Country near Natchitoches have been fairly well known and are sometimes referred to as Free Mulattoes. Comparable people in New Orleans were often called Quadroons, but in the brand book, there was a fine differentiation (see "Cattle Branding in Southwest Louisiana," page 47), *Nègre Libre* (N.L.), *Négresse Libre* (Nsse Libre), *Mulâtre Libre* (M.L.), *Quarteron Libre* (Q.L.), *Griffe Libre* are some of the French appelations. Free man of color (F. M. C.), Free woman of color (F. W. C.), and Colored (Col.) are some of the English designations.

Over the years these people have taken on the ways of their white neighbors. They farm, they take part in horse racing, they speak a variation of the Acadian French dialect, they belong to the Roman Catholic Church, and they maintain their way of life more or less in between their lighter and darker neighbors. As pointed out in the sketch on branding, they still differentiated between themselves and the freedmen after the Civil War. They were proud of their former status, and some of the older colored people recall highlights of their curious pasts. As some of the lighter Negroes and some of the free people of color had come from the Senegal River country in Africa, that is a rather familiar name among colored people in southwest Louisiana. One man of that name said, "There never was a white man named Senegal." And he probably was correct.

Another group, although by no means a major one, came to the vicinity of New Iberia and a nearby lake, since called Spanish Lake. They were Spaniards who came in during the Spanish period, and while their original settlements were not on the prairies, some of them later moved westward and were absorbed into Acadian-French society, even in their language.

ONEZIPHORE GUIDRY, for
many years owner and op-
erator of a *fais-dodo* dance
hall in Rayne.

THE LATE ANATOLE THIBO-
DEAUX, a farmer in Lafay-
ette Parish, was a cheerful
fellow, loved by everyone
who knew him.

The fourth great migration to the prairies came with the settlement of much unclaimed grassland in the western part which
had been used only haphazardly for grazing. Those lands had
been considered too poor and too poorly drained for the growing
of row crops, but beginning in the eighties, they were put to use
for raising rice. The new rice farmers were a distinctive group
from the north-central and eastern states, and they came largely
as a result of nationwide advertising of the area by land companies which were promoting the new business as well as their
own. These people came to make homes on the prairies and to
raise rice just as they had raised wheat in the North. They stood
out in contrast to the Acadians, whom they tended to displace in
certain parts of the prairies.

Another minor group came to the Acadian prairies. They were
Germans who followed the Anglo-Saxon farmers into the rice
country. They settled in greatest numbers in the vicinity of Robert's Cove north of Rayne and in Faquetaïque. Being outnumbered, they soon lost much of their German way of life and were
absorbed mainly into the rice-growing community—some of them
became quite closely associated with their Acadian neighbors.

Some immigrants of French origin settled at the Poste des At-takapas from time to time, and small numbers of them entered the prairie areas as both farmers and as townspeople who estab-lished businesses of their own. This group was not very numerous.

In sociological developments, it seems to be expected that the majority group of any area is to dominate the minority groups and perhaps even absorb them. That is the principle of the so-called American melting pot. We have all become Americans, and we all speak English. But what happened in southwest Lou-isiana where another group, the Acadians, were numerically dominant? Just as one would expect, they became the most im-portant group, and it was they who dominated and even ab-sorbed many of their neighbors. By a process which sociologists call acculturation, the Acadians took in and absorbed hundreds of people from other groups to such an extent that the newcomers lost all contact with their original groups and had no feeling of belonging to any but the Acadian population. Their names and, of course, the memories of older people help to put the story to-gether, case by case.

J. Hanno Deiler, in a study, *The Settlements of the German Coast of Louisiana and the Creoles of German Descent,* printed in 1909, pointed out that the Acadians on the banks of the Mis-sissippi had absorbed the Germans into their own ranks to such an extent that the Germans had even forgotten that they once had been Germans. T. Lynn Smith and Vernon J. Parenton followed up Deiler's work with a study entitled "Acculturation of the Lou-isiana French," published in the *American Journal of Sociology,* November, 1938. In this study the process of absorption is described and analyzed. From what Smith and Parenton said, and from previous observations of my own, it is safe to say that the most certain and effective way of absorbing an outsider into the Acadian way of life came about when an Acadian girl who spoke no language other than Acadian-French was married to an Anglo-Saxon, or a German, or a Spaniard, or an Irishman. Under such circumstances, the power of the Acadian girl was not to be under-estimated, for soon she had her husband speaking Acadian French, and of course she brought the children up to speak the only language that she and her relatives knew. Since there was little opportunity for going to school and not much need for learning to read and write, the Acadian French language sufficed and in another generation no one in the family knew any language other than that of the mother. Today in southwest Louisiana there are Acadians named Stanford, Hanks, Smith, Hoffpauir, Moore, Schexnaidre, Webre, Miguez, Perez, Alleman, Hernandez, and Miller.

There is no way of telling just how much influence the Church and plain conservatism played in the process of acculturation. Usually, the wedding was a church wedding, so there was no question about the religion of the offspring. Natural shyness may have had something to do with it. Since Acadian French bound no one very strictly to rules of grammar, or even vocabulary, it might be assumed that a working knowledge of the language was not very difficult to attain. The evidence would bear that out, however badly the language may be spoken.

Complete settlement of the prairies came, such as it was, before the turn of the century. The filling up of the open lands was a process of fencing in and plowing new fields at the expense of the grasslands. More sugar cane, more cotton, more corn, and more rice with less and less land left in pasture sums it up. The last great breaking of prairie sod was in the plowing up of the central and western Acadian prairies for the planting of rice.

8

The Old Acadian
Cattle Industry

THE *vacherie* of the old Acadians who came to St. Martinville and Opelousas in 1765 became the dominant feature of their early cattle industry. It was to them what a rancho or a hacienda was to Spanish-speaking people of Texas and Mexico. Although the word is French and simply designates a place where one raises cattle, there appears to be no connecting link between the Louisiana system of raising cattle and any comparable system in France. Only in the Camargue in southern France do Frenchmen tend wild cattle, and there never has been any important connection between that section of France and southwest Louisiana.

It usually was from Spanish sources that French Louisiana derived its early stocks of cattle.[1] For this reason a few remarks about

[1]Richard J. Morrisey, "The Northward Expansion of Cattle Ranching in New Spain, 1550-1600," *Agricultural History* (July, 1951), 115-21.

Spanish use and dissemination of cattle may set the stage for a discussion of the early Louisiana cattle industry.

To begin, it must be remembered that there were no cattle in the New World before 1492. The Spanish brought cattle to the West Indies soon after their first explorations. About thirty years later Cortez established a hacienda in Mexico and registered his own cattle brand—the Three Christian Crosses—the oldest cattle brand on the North American continent. With few natural enemies, the industry flourished, and the animals multiplied into tremendous numbers. Thus we see that the Mexican cattle industry was about two centuries older than that of Louisiana.

Early Mexican exploring, mission-founding, and colonizing expeditions which moved northward from the vicinity of Mexico City traveled under organized plans with great herds of livestock. They had horses and mules for transportation, and they had cattle for subsistence and for establishing herds in new territory. A herd of cattle was, in some cases, the commissary department of the expedition. Coronado, more than four hundred years ago, traveled northward from Mexico with a vast herd of livestock, as did other Spanish explorers and colonizers for many decades to come.

The *entradas* into Texas before 1700 were complete and well organized.[2] In the contemporary diaries of those expeditions, there are notes about pack mules being lost and pack mules being found; cattle lost and cattle found.[3] (By getting lost the animals got into the historical record; otherwise they would have gone unrecorded because the expeditions were so commonplace.)

Early Louisiana literature shows that cattle were sought from the Spaniards in Florida, the West Indies, and in Mexico.[4] Col-

[2]Mattie Austin Hatcher, *The Expedition of Don Domingo Teran de los Rios Into Texas, 1691-1692* (Austin, 1932).

[3]Juan Antonio de la Peña, "Diary of the Aguayo Expedition," tr. by Peter P. Forrestal, Texas Catholic Historical Society, *Preliminary Studies*, II, No. 7 (January, 1935).

[4]Lauren C. Post, "The Domestic Animals and Plants of French Louisiana in the Literature With References to Sources, Varieties and Uses," *Louisiana Historical Quarterly*, XVI, No. 4 (1933), 554-86.

onists in Louisiana obtained long-horned cattle from the Spaniards, and to some extent they copied their ways of handling them, particularly in their system of branding. Yet the French-speaking *vacher* never became as proficient at riding and roping as the *vaquero* of the Spanish-speaking areas of Mexico, Texas, New Mexico, and California.

The earliest brands were registered in several books in St. Martinville with the earliest being dated, or perhaps back-dated, at 1739. Entries in the early St. Martinville books are rather irregular, but out of those books came a larger and more systematic volume entitled *Brand Book for the Districts of Attakapas and Opelousas, 1760-1888.*

For part of the story of Acadian cattle raising we are indebted to *History of Agriculture in the Southern United States to 1860,* by Lewis Cecil Gray.[5] This important book, published in 1941, is well documented with early references to cattle grazing in the South, and in it the following contract appears:

In the third quarter of the eighteenth century much of central and southern Louisiana became an important herding region. It is probable that this development was due largely to the Acadians who came to the Province in 1765. An interesting contract made between a colony of Acadians and a Captain Dauterive is preserved. The latter undertook to furnish each Acadian family with five cows with their calves and a bull. During the first year he agreed to run the risk of any losses that might occur, replacing the cattle that died. At the end of six years the Acadians were to return the number originally loaned of the same kind and age and divide half the profits and the increase.

From a decree issued by Don Alexander O'Reilly, governor of Louisiana in 1770, which was printed in B. F. French's *Historical Collections of Louisiana,* we learn that land grants, stock-fencing laws, and branding of cattle all required special attention:

No grant in Opelousas, Attakapas, and Natchitoches shall exceed one league in front by one league in depth; but when the land granted shall not have that depth, a league and a half in front by a league and a half may be granted.

[5](2 vols., New York, 1941), I, 149-50.

To obtain in the Opelousas, Attakapas, and Natchitoches, a grant of forty-two arpents in front by forty-two arpents in depth, the applicant must make it appear that he is the possessor of one hundred head of tame cattle, some horses and sheep, and two slaves to look after them . . . .

Cattle shall be permitted to go at large, from the eleventh of November for one year, to the fifteenth of March of the year following; and at all other times the proprietor shall be responsible for the damage that his cattle may have done to his neighbors.

All cattle shall be branded by the proprietors; and those who shall not have branded them at the age of eighteen months cannot thereafter claim any property.

Nothing can be more injurious to the inhabitants than strayed cattle, without the destruction of which tame cattle cannot increase, and the inhabitants will continue to labor under those evils of which they have so often complained to us; and considering that the province is at present infested with stray cattle, we allow to the proprietors until the 1st day of July, of the next year, one thousand seven hundred and seventy-one, and no longer, to collect and kill, for their use, the said strayed cattle; after which time they shall be considered wild, and may be killed by any person whomsoever, and no one shall oppose himself thereto; or lay claim to any property therein.[6]

Charles Sealsfield, a traveler in the Attakapas country in 1799, showed that the cattle in that country were quite numerous as well as different from the native cattle of France. In his *Cabin Book of Sketches* he wrote the following:

We met a herd of cattle of about a thousand head, among which were about a hundred head of horses of the half-wild Mexican race.

Our cattle in Attakapas differ from those in France very materially by their extraordinary fine horns, which are generally about two and a half feet long, so that with these and their long shanks and feet, when seen from a distance, they look more like deer than like cows and oxen— their usual red-brown color heightens the illusion.[7]

Some years later William Darby, in his *Geographical Description of the State of Louisiana,* likewise showed a Spanish origin

[6]B. F. French, *Historical Collections of Louisiana* (5 vols., New York, 1846-76), V, 290.

[7]Charles Sealsfield, *The Cabin Book of Sketches of Life in the Southwest* (New York, 1844), 252.

for the horses and cattle of the Acadian prairies. After he had done a great deal of field work and surveying in southwest Louisiana, he said: "The cattle, horses, and modes of managing both came into Louisiana from the Spanish provinces in North America. The race of the domestic cow, so greatly multiplied in Opelousas and Attakapas, is high, clean limbed, and elegant in its appearance. The horses are from the Andalusian, or Nubian race; they are, like their ancestors, small, compactly built, and inconceivably durable."[8]

No longer was there any shortage of cattle in Louisiana. There was need only for means of continuing the industry and finding a market for the beef cattle. After settlement of the eastern and potentially more productive portions of the prairies, there was a westward movement across the prairies. First, the settlement pattern followed the French and Spanish systems of granting lands to settlers along the water courses. Grants fronted on the bayous where the woods were located and extended for about forty arpents into the open prairies. Houses were built, usually in the old-time Acadian style, near the woods, and from that time the herds were controlled with a minimum of effort. Herds of different owners ran together *au large,* which to the Acadians meant open prairie. Annual branding and sorting out of animals to be sold took a minimum of time.

The characteristic scene on the old prairies seems to have been the farmstead in which the old steep-roofed Acadian style house was the main feature. About the house would be a few oaks and chinaberry trees, a pen or two made of cypress *pieux,* and a garden and small field. Close to many of the old farmsteads were ponds.

The *chenières,* or oak ridges, in the coastal marsh areas afforded winter grazing for many cattle, and hence called for a type of seasonal movement of cattle. They generally moved into the

[8]William Darby, *A Geographical Description of the State of Louisiana* (New York, 1817), 76.

ACADIAN FARMERS and sharecroppers waiting their turn at a vat where cattle were dipped in the campaign against tick fever in 1934. The state was declared "tick free" in 1936.

marshes for the winter grazing and out in the summer to avoid the mosquitoes.[9]

So far we have dealt only with establishment and nature of cattle raising. Disposing of the cattle naturally was important. Many of them slaughtered at home as beef made an important item of diet for the Acadians and all other inhabitants of southwest Louisiana. New Orleans and the plantations along the Mississippi and along bayous afforded the main commercial markets. There were several routes by which cattle moved eastward. Some herds were gathered and sent overland to Breaux Bridge on Bayou Têche. From there they swung north and crossed the Atchafalaya Basin and reached the Mississippi River in the vicinity of Baton Rouge. Then they went downriver toward New Orleans. Other cattle were driven downstream along the banks of the Têche to Berwick, where they were loaded on large cattle boats. These boats were called "round boats" because they made the trip "around" by way of the Atchafalaya, Red, and Mississippi rivers to New Orleans. On the trip down the Mississippi the boats peddled cattle to the planters along the way, and they usually sold the residue of the loads at New Orleans.

A great many cattle were driven to Washington, on Bayou Courtableau, from which point they were shipped to the Mississippi River markets. Jack Preston, an eighty-two-year-old Negro who was living in Washington in 1935, told of having hauled

[9]Robert E. Williams, "Growing Beef on Marsh Land," *The Cattleman* (November, 1955), 31, 47-48.

cattle from that port to New Orleans by steamboat. He said that the cattle were driven in from the prairies and kept in a big "bull-pen" by the bayou. From there they were loaded on boats that carried between three and four hundred head. He saw twelve or thirteen thousand head a year hauled in the eighties, and the boats took their loads right into New Orleans without stopping to unload any along the way unless they had trouble. An old Opelousas newspaper said that the port of Washington on Bayou Courta-bleau shipped fifteen thousand head of cattle in 1877.[10] Not only were the cattle from Louisiana sold in this way, but many herds from Texas were driven through. They followed the bayous, one of which was the Queue de Tortue, in crossing the prairies. One old-timer said that the Texas cattle were much larger than the Louisiana cattle.

In spite of the apparently rosy picture of a cattle industry in which grass grew well with the abundant rainfall, the industry was not without its handicaps. One was the serious nature of the cold spells of some of the winters. The order and time of occur-rence of the winter phenomena also were negative factors. It is known to local inhabitants that a freeze during a dry spell kills the grass. As previously mentioned, after the grass is killed the heavy winter rains cause it to rot, leaving the cattle without win-ter pasture; on the other hand, rains before the freeze will help to preserve the grass so that there might be grazing during the entire winter. It was the uncertainty of conditions that caused the greatest concern to the *vacherie* owners, yet in early times they did little to protect their cattle against starvation and cold. The sharpness of the cold was particularly destructive to the herds when they were hungry and emaciated. Old-timers recalled that after such spells of cold weather the men were kept busy skinning the dead ones rather than doing anything about the living ones. The bones of thousands of them bleached upon the prairies after the harder winters.

[10]*The Opelousas Courier* (March 9, 1878).

CATTLE RESTING in the shade of moss-covered oaks on the bank of Bayou Vermilion near Abbeville.

Of course there were large owners and small owners, the larger owners on the Opelousas prairies getting the major portion of the publicity in the old days. They hired stock tenders to look after their cattle and supervise the roundups and the branding. Undoubtedly, the large owners crowded the smaller ones. But the small owners retaliated. The stories were that a man seldom ate his own beef. One man looked up at a cow after killing her calf and saw his brand on the cow. He exclaimed, "My God, I killed my own calf!" Inevitably the time came when a man had to eat his own beef.

Almost from its beginning, there were encroachments upon the old cattle industry by more stable forms of agriculture. Naturally such crops as sugar cane and cotton entered from the east, and in time plantation agriculture developed on the Têche and Courtableau bayous as well as on the adjacent grasslands. Plantation agriculture, and also the settlements of small farmers, called for the plowing up of grassland, pushing the open grazing cattle industry a little farther west. Sugar cane and corn grown alternately in sugar country became the main crops in the eastern section. Those two crops continued to dominate considerable areas of the lower alluvial lands, with the recent addition of soy beans.

Then, on the higher lands in the vicinity of Lafayette and Opelousas and in a considerable area immediately to the west, there
developed a region of cotton and corn.[11] This was largely an
area of *petits habitants,* a high percentage of whom were of Acadian ancestry. On their little farms, many of which came to be
about forty acres in extent, every farmer had his own livestock:
horses, mules, cattle, and hogs. The cattle were and still are kept
for beef and milk, and, indeed, in local areas of that section there
are today highly efficient dairy farmers. Other crops, such as
sweet potatoes, have been added. It is likely that any decrease in
numbers of cattle there is much more than compensated for by
improvement in quality.

With the introduction of rice growing in Acadia Parish and
areas to the west came one of the most drastic changes in the
prairie landscapes.[12] In the 1880's and immediately after the building of the Southern Pacific Railroad, some northerners in the
vicinity of Crowley and Jennings conceived the idea of applying
wheat farming methods and techniques to the growing of rice.
With the application of those farm tools for plowing, disking,
harrowing, planting, and harvesting, came the greatest and most
revolutionary changes in rice growing. This story is one of a dra-
matic change, and it is truly an important part of the agricultural
revolution of this country. In time the growing of rice was completely mechanized, and the great and remaining portion of the
prairies was plowed up and planted to the new crop.

The marshlands of the southwest Louisiana coastal area probably have changed less than any area in the raising of cattle.
Since that area is not crop land, its future is quite different from
that of the sugar cane, cotton, and rice country, and its story de-
serves a separate place from that of the other areas.

---

[11]Post, "Acadian Contracts in Southwest Louisiana: Some Sociological Observations," *Rural Sociology,* VI, No. 2 (June, 1941), 144-55.
[12]Post, "The Rice Country of Southwest Louisiana," *The Geographical Review*
(October, 1940), 574-90.

9

Cattle Branding
in Southwest Louisiana

T<small>HE</small> old and the new in cattle branding in southwest Louisiana, is told by two brand books. The first of the books, referred to after this as the "old book," is entitled, "Brand Book for the Districts of Opelousas and Attakapas, 1760-1888." It applied to that general area which later became the parishes of St. Martin, St. Mary, St. Landry, Iberia, Lafayette, Vermilion, Acadia, Calcasieu, and Cameron. This book was presented to the Stephens Memorial Library of the University of Southwestern Louisiana in Lafayette by Mrs. Gradney Cochran when it was superseded by a later book. It was hand written by the many recorders who kept it, with some writing in French and some writing in English. It was never published, but it has been microfilmed.

The "new book" is entitled *Louisiana Brand Book, 1955*. It is the result of the statewide system adopted for recording brands, and this is its second edition. From the title page, the following was copied:

Official Brand Book of the State of Louisiana. This Book Contains All of the Livestock Brands on Record in the State Office at Baton Rouge, Louisiana, Up to the Close of Business on December 31, 1954 . . . issued by the Department of Agriculture and Immigration, Livestock Brand Commission of Louisiana at Baton Rouge.

In the old book there are more than 25,000 separate recordings of brands. In the new there are about 30,000, but with the added supplement, there are recorded for the state of Louisiana more than 32,000 active brands. A third edition was released in 1960.

General interest in brands the country over and the lack of information about the subject, suggested to the writer that some descriptive and historical background would be appropriate here. Hence this brief sketch on branding, brands, the reading of brands, brand laws, and brand inspections in Louisiana.

Drawings in Egyptian tombs show that cattle have been branded for thousands of years.[1] Nevertheless, no better method of marking cattle than branding with a hot iron has been discovered. Ear marking, horn branding, and branding with acid are all unsatisfactory. The burnt brand is a permanent mark that can be seen from a distance, and even months after a stolen steer has been slaughtered the branded hide may stand in court as legal identification of the animal. At branding time many a stockman has said, "Burn it on good boys. She will wear it all of her life."

Most branding irons are stamping irons with which the brand is put on with one impression. The running iron, by contrast, is a hooked iron with which one can simply write his brand on a calf. Formerly, all cattle were roped and thrown to be branded, but nowadays only calves are thrown. Grown cattle are branded in chutes, and large-scale calf branding is done with squeeze chutes and tables. There is a saying that Mexicans use a short-

[1]Oren Arnold and John P. Hale, *Hot Irons* (New York, 1944), 28. These authors refer to the Oriental Institute of the University of Chicago as authority for evidence of branding at least 2000 B.C.

St. Martin C.

FACSIMILE REPRODUCTION of page 113 of the "Brand Books for the Districts of Opelousas and Attakapas, 1760-1888." These brands appear to have been copied from the older St. Martinville books after the brand office was removed to Lafayette in 1824. Note that the old-style French way of writing some of the months was used. *7bre* for September and *8bre* for October. It is likely that the Ozene family brand was ID and the children added numbers to make their own individual brands.

Brand	Owner	Brand	Owner
10/7	Boutté Louis Hilaire, homme de couleur libre, St. Martin Jan. 17, 1817, p. 13	ⱦ (X crossed)	Chevallier Declouet St. Martin, June 1, 1780 p. 40
ⱨB	Paul Pierre Briant St. Martin, July 20, 1821 p. 15	Œ+	Declouet Chevalier fils d'Alexandre, St. Martin June 18, 1784, p. 43
☆ (cross over star)	Briant Pierre Paul St. Martin, Oct. 9, 1824 p. 15	n4	Martin Duralde St. Martin, Mar. 12, 1789 p. 46
Jꜩb	Louis Maduse (Spaniard) St. Martin, July 14, 1827 p. 17	mo	Modist Delahousay, FWC St. Martin, July 12, 1814 p. 47
JPL	Catin, Negresse Libre passed to Louis La Violette, June 13 1808, St. Martin, p. 24	⚔ (crossed axes)	François Quarteron Libre St. Martin, May 29, 1792 p. 57
ꝋs (O-s with cross)	Celestin Sauvage Attakapas St. Landry, June 13, 1808 p. 24	5F	Louis Grevemberg St. Martin, Oct. 14, 1793 p. 64
2b⁴	Celestin Sauvage Attakapas St. Martin, Aug. 18, 1804 p. 29	FR	Francois Grevemberg St. Martin, Oct. 14, 1770 p. 64
ⵣ (cross symbol)	Chaulinette Quarteron Libre St. Martin, Aug. 12, 1805 p. 30	Z3	Josephe, Mitif Libre St. Martin, Aug. 4, 1800 p. 81
I°N	Charlotte Nsse Libre St. Martin, July 26, 1815 p. 33	Ꝺ	Jos. Mathew, Griffe Libre, St. Landry, Oct. 7, 1822, p. 98
JⱢ	Chataign Sauvage St. Martin, 1826 p. 33	ⱳ	Melançon Veuve St. Martin, Sept. 21, 1801 p. 105
PS	Dermancourt Joseph Sauvage St. Landry, Aug. 4, 1825 p. 38	⊿ (arrow shape)	Belthazare Martel St. Martin, July 16, 1823 p. 108
D͓C×̣	Chavalier Declouet St. Martin, June 1, 1770 p. 40	ID	Ozenne père St. Martin, Oct. 14, 1748 p. 113
D͓C×̣	Declouet Vve. St. Martin, June 1, 1776 p. 40	I²D	Ozenne Marie St. Martin, Aug. 11, 1802 p. 113
GP	Gansalan Deprados St. Martin, Mar. 1, 1780 p. 40	ID7	Ozenne Usin son fils St. Martin, Sept. 11, 1802 p. 113

SOME BRANDS from the "Brand Book for the Districts of Opelousas and Attakapas, 1760-1888." The format used here is that of the modern *Louisiana Brand Book, 1955*. Note that early recordings are in French, and the later ones in English. Indians and colored people usually were listed by a single name.

Brand	Owner	Brand	Owner
FXM	F. X. Martin St. Martin, Sept. 1, 1823 p. 108	P	Gilbert Handy, fils freedman, St. Landry, Aug. 28, 1866, p. 407
℞	Alexander Porter St. Martin, Aug. 16, 1809 p. 118	ⵡ	Marie Thibodeaux freedwoman, St. Martin July 29, 1867, p. 421
WK	William Wikoff St. Landry, June 29, 1815 p. 150	ⵜ	Edmond Senegal, col. Lafayette, July 31, 1869 p. 443
≠	Lenlotte f.w.c. St. Martin, Aug. 23, 1830 p. 168	⌂	Philomène Gautraut Lafayette, Nov. 16, 1872 p. 494
X̌	Marie Louise Senegal, f.w.c. Lafayette, Apr. 9, 1840 p. 217	+3	John McNeese Calcasieu, Nov. 29, 1873 p. 501
SUC	Sebastian Hernandez Lafayette, April 10, 1844 p. 237	WARE	John M. Ware St. Landry, May 25, 1883 p. 588
ᴕᴕ	John Hanks Vermilion, Aug. 27, 1844 p. 240	ⵘ	Joseph Jefferson Iberia, July 21, 1887 p. 613
ꞮϽ	Desiré Miguez St. Martin, Aug. 21, 1857 p. 279	4D	Domingue Ceasar Acadia, June 13, 1888 p. 618
Sⱦ	Sosthène Schixnayder Vermilion, Sept. 10, 1855 p. 310	4O	Joseph Breaux Acadia, June 13, 1888 p. 618
Hλ	Louis Attakapas St. Landry p. 332	4⫪	Alphonse Broussard St. Martin, June 14, 1888 p. 618
♡	Baptiste Mulatre Libre St. Landry, Sept. 4, 1815 p. 338	4K	Geo. K. Bradford Acadia, Aug. 29, 1888 p. 620
▽	Arm Duhon Lafayette, Mar. 31, 1882 p. 578	∂H	Aladin Hanks Acadia, Aug. 11, 1888 p. 620
Ⴗ	Joseph Greene Senegal, f.m.c Lafayette, Aug. 15, 1866 p. 406	4H	Levigne Comeaux Acadia, July 21, 1888 p. 619
♡	Leocadie St. André, f.p.c. St. Landry, Aug. 30, 1866 p. 407	42	Alcide Richard Lafayette, June 30, 1888 p. 619

ADDITIONAL BRANDS from the "Brand Book, 1760-1888." Gilbert Handy, *fils* freedman, shows as being transitional. The great majority of listings were those of white cattlemen; these are among the unusual designations and may be of interest for a variety of reasons.

Brand	Owner	Brand	Owner
W	Noah Ward 6821 Government St. Baton Rouge	ᴸA	La. State Penitentiary Angola
L	Earl K. Long Winfield	ᴸu	Animal Indus. Dept. LSU Univ. Station Baton Rouge
⌣P	David L. Pearce Oak Grove	N⅗	Martin Petitjean 503 N. Adams Ave. Rayne
FD	Dupré Credeur Rt. 1, Box 521 Duson	SP	La. State Police Baton Rouge
⊤C	Dr. Martin O. Miller 912 Pere Marquette New Orleans	—LS	Southwestern La. Inst. Lafayette
△	J. M. Petitjean 131 Harrison St. Lake Charles	C+C	St. Charles College Grand Coteau
⚚	J. Warren Arceneaux Rt. 1, Box 127 Rayne	✝	St. Gertrude's Convent Ramsey
Fc	Fernest Faulk 410 West Third St. Kaplan	⊣E	J. Earl Stutes Box 5 Duson
◇M	R. Watkins Greene R. F. D. Youngsville	HP	Harry Post Luling
F⌐	Wilfred Falcon Rt. 1, Box 155 F Rayne	Ⓓ	Alcide Dominique Box 940 Lafayette
EP	Dr. Elmo E. Petitjean 303 West Lessley Rayne	$	Swift and Co. Box 991 Lake Charles
⋉W	B. K. Whitfield Box 173 Lafayette	4K	Chas. M. Bradford Rayne
⊞	Mrs. Rayme Boudreaux J. B. Route Cameron	M	Aubrey J. Marceau Box 184 Kaplan
I◎H	John A. Heinen 1005 N. Polk Rayne	—∧—	Mrs. Agnes Tanner Box 103 Duson

SOME BRANDS from the *Louisiana Brand Book, 1955.* These are modern Louisiana brands, usually with some meaning or sentiment involved in simple patterns. The letters, R and L, indicate the side on which the animal is branded.

handled iron and get on their knees to brand, while Anglo-Americans use a long-handled iron and stand while using the iron. If there is any validity to the saying, it might be explained by the fact that the Americans are much more inclined than the Mexicans to use chutes for branding.

Styles or patterns of brands tend to vary with different people and places. At the meeting grounds of the Latin and Anglo-Americans in Texas and the rest of the Southwest, the Mexican brands were referred to here and there as "crazy Mexican brands, maps of Mexico, greazer madhouses, and skillets of snakes."[2] They were brands with complicated crooked and curved lines and many curlicues. They were brands that couldn't be read. No wonder there was a *Quién Sabe* brand!

As evidenced by the folklore of the western cattle country, cowboys developed reputations for picturesque speech, and out of that speech came much of the terminology that is used today in reading brands. Those expressions give color and atmosphere to what might sound dull and uninteresting. Who else would have thought of the Pig Pen, Buzzard on a Rail, Dog Iron, Long Rail, Pitch Fork, Hay Fork, Hash Knife, Flying V, and Running W? Other famous names merely say what they are, such as the Four Sixes, Maltese Cross, 101, and XIT.

Brands are read from left to right, from top to bottom, or from outside in. The 101, Bar BQ (with the bar over the B and Q), and the Circle D afford clear examples of how to read brands aloud. For systematic recording, a somewhat similar pattern is followed. The cowboys' names for brands have become more or less official, but naturally there are some variations from place to place. With little difficulty and in a few moments one can draw twenty-four or more different H brands. Among them would be the H, Lazy H, Tumbling H, Walking H, Running H, Drag H, Flying H, Rafter H, Rocking H, Quarter Circle H, Circle H, Box H, and Swinging H. Since the cattleman chooses his own brand, provided

---

[2]*Ibid.;* Ramon F. Adams, *Western Words* (Norman, 1944).

the brand is not already in use, an almost endless number of styles of brands will be seen in any brand book.

The perfect brand is easy to make and difficult to blot. In looking over the brands in the old and new books, it is obvious that the newer brands are the more sophisticated (see page 52). Usually they are simpler and have more meaning, part of which may be an expression of sentiment.

Old southwest Louisiana brands showed that sentiment played little part in their design. Many of them look like Mexican and Argentine brands. Certainly, designs and names of brands could not have been as important as they were later in the Old West, where the whole outfit went by the name of the brand, and where today the brand might be seen on the chimney stack, the barn, the front gate, the cars, the trucks, oil rigs, and equipment, and even on the bank checks. There it has become the cattleman's symbol, comparable to a trademark—the heraldry of the range.

As an example of how little sentiment went into the planning or designing of brands of the old book, there are in the last few pages no fewer than forty brands which are variations of the number 4. One of them is the 4HK of George G. Bradford of Acadia Parish. The same brand appears again in the new book, having been registered by Mr. Bradford's son, Charles M. Bradford of Rayne. The brand remained as family property, but obviously sentiment played no part in the original designing of the forty brands which were listed for different parishes and under unrelated names. Also, some of those brands could scarcely have had very attractive-sounding names (see page 51). Other brands that appear in different series obviously are those of families. The father had the old brand, and his sons each took the same brand but added a number to it. This undoubtedly simplified identification of the family stock.

Brand laws are set by the states, not by the federal government. They vary from state to state, but it might be noted that usually they were initiated or put through the various state legislatures by cattlemen and their organizations. It might be noted also that in cattle country, which of course includes Louisiana, cattlemen are very prominent among the legislators, even though some of them may be "gentlemen or part-time cattlemen." Therefore it would be expected that livestock brand and inspection laws would be devised to give the cattleman the benefit of the increase of his herd.

These points gleaned from various places show the tenor of different brand laws:

1. No branding is to be done between sundown and sunup. (In other words, no moonlight branding jobs.)

2. No branding to be done outside a corral.

3. No brands are to be altered.

4. No branding is to be done with a running iron. (In some cases it is illegal to possess a running iron.)

5. All cattle are to be inspected when they are sold or when they are moved from one brand district to another. (In some cases they must be inspected when they are moved from one county to another.)

6. No inspection between sundown and sunup, or by artificial light. (In other words, no moonlight inspection jobs.)

7. Cattle in a truck must be unloaded to be inspected—except in case there is only one head in the truck.

The various states and the cattlemen's organizations maintain inspectors at places such as stockyards, shipping points, auction yards, and on the highways, to check brands in a continuous war against cattle thieves and to find lost or strayed cattle. The war is not just a local one; it operates on a nationwide basis.

The venting of brands is not widely practiced, nor is it generally understood. The word comes from the Mexican *venta* meaning sale, but in practice it has come to mean nullification of previous brands, or a counter-branding *(contramarca)* which voids the first one. In Argentina the seller rebrands the cattle he sold but with his iron inverted.[3] It appears that Mexican and other western cattlemen had a special vent brand with which they nullified the original brand.

Various historical references tell of horses and mules bearing Mexican brands although they were hundreds, perhaps even thousands, of miles from the ranchos where they were bred. So long as they never returned to Mexico, little more was ever said of the stock. However, complications sometimes arose. Gregg and Webb, who were Santa Fe traders, both mentioned the need for having brands properly vented.[4] Their cases were unusual, in that they took mules back into the country of their origin. Mules that were stolen by Comanche Indians on their raids down into Chihuahua and Durango were sold to traders who in turn sold them to the Santa Fe traders to be used on their wagon trains. As the wagons entered the different Mexican towns on the southward expeditions, brand inspectors with their irons tied to their saddles rode up and down the trains inspecting brands. Any mule bearing one of their irons (*hierro*) was confiscated, and he had to be purchased a second time.

Inspectors stationed at Cajon Pass in California were supposed to inspect all horses leaving California over the Old Spanish Trail to see that their brands were properly vented.[5] (It is quite likely that when Pegleg Smith and other mountain men carried out their bigger raids on the California missions and ranchos, there was little time for inspecting the vast herds that were stolen.)

A vent or counterbrand was a useful device in Attakapas even as early as 1774. Alexandro Caballero Declouet, captain and lieutenant-governor of Attakapas, in 1774 sent Señor Grevemberg, captain of the militia of Attakapas, and three soldiers to San An-

[3]Tito Saubidet, *Vocabulario y Refranero Criollo* (2d ed., Buenos Aires, 1945), 105.
[4]Josiah Gregg, "Commerce of the Prairies, or Journal of a Santa Fe Trader," *Early Western Travels*, 1748-1846, ed. by R. G. Thwaites (Cleveland, 1905), XIX, 320; James Josiah Webb, *Adventures in the Santa Fe Trade* ("Southwest Historical Series," Ralph P. Bieber, ed. [Glendale, 1931]), 1, 192.
[5]Leroy R. and Ann W. Hafen, *Old Spanish Trail, Santa Fe to Los Angeles* ("The Far West and Rockies Historical Series, 1820-1875" [Glendale, 1954]), 1, 244.

tonio, Texas, to buy horses and mules at that post. As there was great suspicion and rivalry between the two colonies, even though both were Spanish at the time, the French were on their very best behavior when traveling in Texas, and especially when on missions for buying horses and mules which were in great demand in New Orleans. It was on that mission that Declouet insisted that the Texas governor designate a counterbrand or mark for venting any previous brands on the stock that was bought. "Your honor will please order all animals sent out of the jurisdiction of that government to be counterbranded, or branded, in order that I may be enabled to confiscate those in the territory under my command which are found without this mark, the lack of which will be sufficient to indicate them as stolen, in which case I shall have the honor to advise your lordship of it."[6]

In the several letters written, the French were most agreeable and, in one case, indicated that Indians had stolen horses from the Texan Spaniards to sell to the Louisiana French. By requiring that the animals be branded with a vent brand, as Declouet pointed out, the practice could be stopped. At that time there was little need for bringing Texas cattle into Louisiana, but the demand for Mexican horses and Texas and Mexican mules continued until a later time. A bill of sale to show that the cattle were acquired legally generally makes venting unnecessary today.

With the preceding background, we shall now turn to Louisiana and to southwest Louisiana more specifically. As previously pointed out, the cattle industry had an early beginning in that section of the state and by the time of the transfer of Louisiana from France to Spain, the industry was flourishing. The Spaniards, however, attempted to put the industry on a systematic basis.

The Spanish governor, Don Alexander O'Reilly, in laying down new laws for Louisiana at New Orleans, on February 18, 1770, paid particular attention to those areas designated as Ope-

---

[6]Charles Wilson Hackett, *Pichardo's Treatise on the Limits of Louisiana and Texas* (Austin, 1941), III, 467.

lousas, Attakapas, and Natchitoches which were recognized as cattle country. He decreed that all "cattle shall be branded by the proprietors; those who shall not have been branded at the age of eighteen months cannot thereafter claim any property therein."[7]

But the cattle industry in southwest Louisiana was much older than that, and so was cattle branding in that section. Two old leatherbound brand books in the courthouse in St. Martinville record earlier brands, and they seem to have been the basis for the recording of all brands in southwest Louisiana until 1824.[8]

In that year, by legislative act, the office of the brand recorder was moved from St. Martinville to Lafayette, and apparently that law resulted in the new "Brand Book for the Districts of Opelousas and Attakapas, 1760-1888."

As might be expected, with a long succession of brand recorders working over a period of sixty-four years and for a period which extended over 128 years, the work had many inconsistencies. At least, they appear to be inconsistencies. One page of a St. Martinville book shows that Louis Grevemberg registered his 5F brand in 1737.[9] In another place the same book shows that he registered the same brand in 1739. The book for 1760-1888 listed Louis Grevemberg as registering the 5F brand on October 14, 1793 (see page 51).

When the recorders copied from the St. Martinville books into the Lafayette book, an attempt was made at alphabetizing names by parishes, a practice which sooner or later became confusing. Other sections of the book are quite unsystematic. How the recorders avoided duplication of brands is difficult to understand. Certainly, much of the information was carried in their heads, as there is no complete alphabetical list of names, nor is there any arrangement of brands such as a brand inspector or reader would expect to find in such a book.

[7]B. F. French, *Historical Memoirs of Louisiana from the First Settlement of the Colony to the Departure of Governor O'Reilly in 1770* (New York, 1853), V, 290.

[8]Noah Ward, "Livestock Brand Inspection in Louisiana," *Gulf Coast Cattleman* (March, 1955), 21.

[9]*Ibid.*

With all of its shortcomings, there are many redeeming features in the book. For each brand registered, the parish of residence of the owner was given, and so was the date of registry. Race was not listed for those who were white, and little is said of the white registrants except for certain Spaniards, although most Spaniards were not so designated. Chavelier Declouet was of French nobility and listed merely as Chavelier Declouet.

It was the Indians and Negroes who received a special designation. As Louisiana French people had no other way of designating Indians, they called them *sauvages*. In all, only about a half-dozen Indians were listed, but one of them had two brands (see page 50). Louisianians had many ways of designating the different Negro mixtures. Among them were the following, all of whom were free before the Civil War: *Nègre Libre, Négresse Libre, Mulâtre Libre, Mulâtresse Libre, Quarteron Libre, Griffe Libre, Mitif Libre, petit nègre, homme de couleur libre, femme de couleur libre, H.C.L., f.c.l.* The f.p.c., f.m.c., and f.w.c. obviously were American abbreviations.

The colored people who were free before the Civil War called themselves Free People of Color, a practice which they continued even after the war. A facsimile reproduction from a page in a Texas brand book for 1872 listed two cattlemen as f.m.c., so the practice apparently was followed also in Texas.[10] Naturally, the freed slaves were called freedmen, and they were so listed. By estimate there were several hundred Free People of Color and several hundred freedmen who registered cattle brands in the old book.

From the 25,000 or more brands in the old book, little can be done on a statistical basis. The parishes changed, brands were transferred, some were nullified, and there was great duplication of names. As the brands passed along from one generation to the next, the statistics would become complicated and would mean little.

[10]Dee Brown, *Trail Driving Days* (New York, 1952), 49.

Local families undoubtedly have kept the same brands for many decades. Some of them point with pride to names of ancestors recorded with their brands. The writer recognized two brands, that of George K. Bradford of Acadia Parish, and that of Arm Duhon of Lafayette. He also recognized in the book the names of several former neighbors, Preston Hoffpauir, Aladdin Hanks, and Adonis Breaux.

The F. X. Martin listed is said to be François-Xavier Martin, noted judge and author of a history of Louisiana. The Alexander Porter listed probably was the noted Whig senator who, like Martin, owned a plantation in the Têche country.[11] The Joseph Jefferson may be the actor who created the role of Rip Van Winkle on the New York stage, for he spent eighteen seasons on his plantation at Jefferson Island, which was named for him.[12] Dozens and even hundreds of prominent names, such as those of William Wikoff and Martin Duralde, are recorded with their brands, but this writer has no basis for checking on them, a point which merely proves the writers of their biographies and their biographical notes knew or cared little about old cattle brands.

For the modern reader the old book records the folkways of selecting, designing, and recording brands. No person other than the recorder could possibly have known or checked all of the contents of the book. It was inadequate for modern times.

Following the era when brands for all of southwest Louisiana were recorded in the old book, there was a period when Louisiana brands were recorded on a parish basis. The various clerks of court recorded their brands locally. Under this system, or lack thereof, it was possible to have sixty-four separate brand books and as many duplications of the same brand. Cattle rustling was rampant, and there was no systematic or legal basis for checking it. With the beginning of the modern cattle industry following

[11]See Wendell Holmes Stephenson, *Alexander Porter, Whig Planter of Old Louisiana* (Baton Rouge, 1934).
[12]See Joseph Jefferson, *The Autobiography of Joseph Jefferson* (New York, 1889), Ch. XVII.

tick eradication in 1936, a new set of laws, a new brand recording system, and a new system of brand inspection were needed.

The modernization of the state laws for preventing cattle stealing followed a normal course of development. The Louisiana Cattlemen's Association, aroused at the stealing that went on during World War II, set to work to correct the situation. J. D. Cooper, a member from Natchitoches who had lived in South Dakota and who was acquainted with the inspection system of that state, helped initiate interest in establishing the new system in Louisiana. Several unsuccessful attempts to get the state legislature to enact laws setting up a brand and inspection system failed, but with long and persistent work by J. D. Cooper, Arthur Gayle, Leslie A. Cowlie, P. T. Sartwelle, A. R. McBurney, Bill Kingrey, E. O. Daughenbaugh, Chester Hyde, and others, the bill was passed in 1944.

At that time there was no one in the state who had the necessary experience in setting up a brand-recording system, nor did anyone realize the immensity of the job. Noah Ward, who had been Chief Quarantine Inspector for the Livestock Sanitary Board for twenty-four years, volunteered to do the recording of the brands for the Livestock Brand Commission. This was most fortunate for Louisiana cattlemen, for Ward not only supplied the well-directed and energetic leadership for getting the job done, but he patterned the Louisiana system after what really amounts to a national system of recording and inspecting brands.

After considerable correspondence with the executive secretaries of brand commissions of many western states, Ward decided to spend some time in Alliance, Nebraska, studying the recording system of that state. Chase Feagins, Secretary and Chief Brand Inspector for the Nebraska Brand Committee, worked unselfishly with Ward in showing him their system. Later Ward attended a meeting of the American National Cattlemen's Association in Denver and was made a member of the Brand and Theft Committee. Here he met with livestock brand law enforcement officers of all states having brand inspection systems. Through such meetings and co-operation it has been possible for Louisiana to have the same system of recording brands and inspecting cattle at sales and slaughter houses as nineteen other states and one Canadian province. Executive secretaries and other officials of the different brand commissions attend meetings of state and national cattlemen's associations where they have the opportunity of studying ways and means of revising the laws and improving their operation so as to stay ahead of the rustlers.

Educational work among livestock owners became a part of the program. The six years between 1944 and 1950 were spent in preliminary work and recording brands, and the first brand book for any southern state appeared in 1950. Not only did the new brand inpsectors learn to read brands, but they learned much about the ways of cattle rustlers. Co-operation with brand inspectors of Texas and those newly appointed inspectors in Mississippi increased the effectiveness of the law.

The Livestock Brand Commission, which was incorporated into and made a part of the Department of Agriculture of the state, began functioning in a prompt and energetic manner. Some cattle thieves were immediately apprehended, tried and convicted, and given mandatory penitentiary sentences. Cattlemen, are continually reminded of the importance of reporting their losses with complete descriptions of the missing stock and their brands to the executive secretary in Baton Rouge. The secretary immediately warns all sheriffs, auction barns, and livestock brand inspectors to inspect their records for the described stock. As might be expected, promptness is essential and any missing cattle handled through the auction barns are apt to be discovered.[13]

Another factor which makes the system all the more effective is that rewards are constantly offered by the different cattlemen's associations for information leading to conviction of cattle thieves.

[13]Ward, "Future Looks Dark for Cattle Thieves," *Gulf Coast Cattleman* (February, 1951) 23.

There has been repeated demand by the cattlemen for more inspectors and means of covering rural areas more completely.[14] The ways of the cattle rustlers of the Old West have changed. They have been supplanted by the rifle, the pickup truck, and the home freezer. On the other hand, the twenty-four brand inspectors are commissioned under the state police, and many are equipped with modern means of communication such as police radios. Although there have been many convictions of cattle thieves, it is likely that a far greater benefit has come to cattlemen through what the system has prevented in the way of stealing.

That the cattlemen are appreciative of the efforts of the commission and other officials is shown by a resolution made public in the April, 1954, issue of the *Gulf Coast Cattleman,* which is the official publication of the Louisiana Cattlemen's Association. The resolution is quoted here only in part:

WHEREAS, the Livestock Brand Commission has done a commendable job in registering cattle brands and issuing a brand book, and

WHEREAS, this agency has cooperated with the livestock industry of the state in every way possible,

THEREFORE BE IT RESOLVED, that we express our thanks and appreciation to the brand commission and its Administrative officer for the excellent service they have given the livestock industry of Louisiana.[15]

With a cattle industry that is changing at a revolutionary pace, the state is fortunate in having a modern system of branding, one which other southern states might do well to emulate.

The new brand book is entirely different from its predecessors; it was compiled and edited by Noah Ward, executive secretary of the Livestock Brand Commission and is a completely systematic work. It is arranged so that anyone skilled in the reading of brands can locate and identify ownership of any of the more than

[14]Ward, "More Brand Inspectors Needed to Cope With Deep Freeze Rustlers," *Gulf Coast Cattleman* (April, 1956), 26.

[15]"Resolutions Adopted at the 12th Annual Convention, Louisiana Cattlemen's Association, Alexandria, La., February 18-19, 1954." Published in the *Gulf Coast Cattleman* (April, 1954), 22.

thirty thousand brands in a few minutes time. Here are some notes from the preface of the book which show, at least in part, how Mr. Ward arranged the order of brands:

> As far as possible, the brands of this book have been arranged alpha-betically; first under letters, second, figures, and last, under characters. Those beginning with characters are arranged as follows: Bars, slashes, quarter circles, crosses, hearts, diamonds, squares, *et cetera*.
>
> The single letters appear first in their different forms, then two letter brands follow, *et cetera*. A brand such as A2 will be found im-mediately after AZ. Letters with bars to the right such as A- will follow A9, after which will be found the three story brands.

The book is in two sections, the first has the brands in systematic order with the owners' names and addresses. The second has all owners' names in alphabetical order with references to pages and places where corresponding brands are found. Thus, one using the book can quickly check brands against names or names against brands.

Still another advantage of the new book over the old is that it is published, and Louisiana law requires that copies of it be sent to all sheriffs, brand inspectors, and clerks of court in the state. Anyone who wishes may purchase a copy of the book by order-ing it from the executive secretary of the Louisiana Brand Com-mission at Baton Rouge. Under the old system, there was only the one hand-written copy of the book, and the recorder sometimes kept the book at his residence.

The new book shows that people of Acadian descent still domi-nate the cattle industry of southwest Louisiana. In a frequency count the name of Broussard leads all others with 340 brands un-der that name. Next in order come these with their frequencies as listed: Fontenot, 337; Miller, 275; Hebert, 259; Trahan, 218; Guil-lory, 210; Smith, 205; Richard, 193; Johnson, 189; Guidry, 157; Theriot, 145; LeBlanc, 139; Jones, 98; and Thibodeaux, 92. Of the 340 Broussard brands, more than 300 were registered from southwest Louisiana.

10

The Sugar Cane
and Corn Country

FARMING often fol-
lows cattle raising, and that is what happened in southwest Louisiana. Three main commercial crops were developed, and each
became distinctive in a certain region and each evidenced certain
characteristics all its own. The three crops, of course, were sugar
cane, cotton, and rice, but of the three none stood alone as a single
crop. With sugar cane, the planters alternated corn; the cotton
farmers alternated cotton and corn in their country; and in the
rice country, they developed a system of alternating rice and cattle
grazing.

Let us deal first with the sugar cane country, as it was oldest
and it seems to have been the most spectacular crop during the
early years. The first successful granulation of sugar from Louisiana cane was accomplished by Étienne de Boré at his plantation in
1795 on the Mississippi. This accomplishment started sugar pro-

duction on its prosperous way on many south Louisiana plantations. Although cane was far more characteristic of the Recent
Alluvial Lands than of the prairies proper, it did penetrate into
the prairies and occupied a considerable amount of grassland
country. Much has been written about sugar production in Louisiana, and most of it would apply to the Attakapas country. On
Bayou Têche the main fields were developed on the natural levees,
particularly those that were not wooded. Although cane would
grow on the backlands and out on the prairies well beyond the
present region of sugar cane, the yields were lighter and supplies
of fuel for sugar making were harder to come by. Early newspapers told of the increase in production of sugar in rather glow-
ing accounts: "In 1825, the Parish of St. Mary produced from two
thousand and nineteen acres of cane, two thousand two hundred
and fifty-four hogsheads of sugar employing seven hundred and
fifty hands." Twenty-two years later, in 1847, another account in
the same newspaper said: "There are numerous fine plantations
on both sides of the bayou [Têche] and nowhere in the state is
it believed that more skill has directed, or greater success has attended the culture of cane than here. This country, though com-
paratively new, produced in 1846, 37,144 hhds. of sugar of 1,000
pounds each."

Statistics showed that in 1854 St. Martin Parish had a great
predominance of Creole planters over "American" planters, whereas the opposite was the case in St. Landry Parish. Where American planters predominated, so did steam mills exceed horse mills
in numbers. Growth continued uninterruptedly until the Civil
War. As indicated previously, sugar cane has always been raised
more readily on the banks of Bayou Têche and the neighboring
areas than on the bluff lands toward Lafayette and on the prairies
proper. All statistics seem to have been for entire parishes, but
there is no doubt that when a parish lay both in lower alluvial
lands and the prairies, most of the production of sugar was on
the lower lands. The statistics further indicated that it was nearer

the bayous such as the Têche that steam mills came to predominate, whereas on the prairies fuel (whether it was wood or imported coal) was so scarce that most of the mills were horse mills. The use of horse mills may also indicate smaller scale operations.

For Lafayette Parish, a list of sugar planters included seven American names and twenty-seven Acadian names. When railroads came to Lafayette Parish, cane derricks and switches were built along them for the loading of cane so that it would be hauled to central refineries. The *St. Landry Democrat* of June 10, 1893, told how a transportation system affected that parish. It pictured the setting of the sugar cane plantations and the terms and conditions in which the people along the Têche thought and lived:

Colossal liveoaks, centuries old, all bearded with moss, lined along the Têche lend to its great scenery a majestic aspect. The country on both banks is high, the soil is light and mellow, fertile beyond expression. Cotton, cane, corn, and all kinds of semi-tropical plants come there with a luxuriant growth, cane yielding as much as four thousand pounds to the acre. Palatial residences range along its shores, especially in the Parish of St. Mary, and ease and comfort are everywhere displayed in that section. Immense central sugar factories turn out vast quantities of sugar, white as snow, some of them as much as five millions of pounds. Their capacities are increasing and improving every day and there is no telling where they will stop. Cane is sold to these factories by the ton at prices ranging from three to five dollars, and the construction of railroads and branches of railroads enable the planters to send them at considerable distances, the price of hauling being generally 25 cents a ton.

Some of the factories have their own railroads. Prof. Knapp, a banker and millionaire of Lake Charles, is now constructing in the upper portion of St. Martin, between Breaux Bridge and Arnaudville, a railroad that will start from Huron plantation on the Têche in the town of St. Peter, in the parish of Lafayette, there to connect with other lines.

Both sides of the Têche, in the rear, are immense forests of valuable woods, of easy access. The sugar planters in the olden times employed this wood as fuel, but since the system of factories has been so solidly established, they find it more to their advantage to burn coal. The coal is towed to the factories in large barges at a reasonable price, and mountains of it can be seen at each factory.

From the above it is obvious that sugar cane was the crop of the rich alluvial lands along the main bayous. It called for great investments and great risks, but during times of prosperity the possibilities for profits were great. Since labor was a very important factor on the sugar plantations, it was the sugar planters who maintained the large number of slaves in Attakapas. The Opelousas country favored cotton, and there it was the cotton planter who brought in the slaves.

There are two aspects of the sugar cane country. The modern aspect has to do with science. It deals with the improvement of varieties of cane to make them more productive, hardier, and more resistant to disease. It deals with the use of chemicals and, particularly, commercial fertilizers. It deals with the mechanization of large-scale harvesting and grinding cane; the use of vacuum boilers rather than open kettles; the use of coal, oil, gas, and electricity in the mills; the use of trucks instead of carts and wagons; and also the displacement of mules with tractors.

But there are traces of the old, leisurely methods to be seen in many places. The plantation houses, with bells which once set the workers to their tasks or told them when it was quitting time are reminders of the old days. Carts and wagons are to be seen here and there, but still more conspicuous is the old iron open kettle which was used long ago for boiling cane juice and making sugar. Today those kettles, long since replaced by the vacuum system of making sugar, are used as water troughs for cattle. They still indicate distribution of the old sugar industry, as they seldom were moved far from their original sites.

The passing of the mule on the cane plantation is another notable change. Formerly the cane planters had the biggest mules used in agriculture in the state. They weighed twelve to fifteen hundred pounds and were fully twice as heavy as the little home-grown Creole mules of the cotton section. These mules were brought in from Missouri and other mule-producing states to the north. "Sugar mules" had to be big. The cane planters plowed deep in the heavy alluvial soils, and the work of cultivating was laborious as was the job of hauling during harvest time.

Until tractors replaced mules on the sugar cane plantations, corn was the main crop rotated or alternated with cane. Cane and corn are both row crops, and no great difficulty was experienced in alternating the crops except for the fact that the cane had to be grown for several consecutive years on the same land. This came about because of the method of planting cane. First, one plants cane stalks by laying them in opened trenches which are then covered perhaps six inches deep. The eyes on the joints of the cane sprout and grow and the cane is then cultivated in rows just about as one would cultivate any other row crop in the south. When the cane is too big to cultivate any longer, it is big enough to shade out weeds, and it is "laid-by" as one lays by corn.

However, for the second cane crop, the planter relies upon the stubbles of the first. He need not plant new cane, but after several years the cane must be renewed by the actual planting of new stalks. Hence the rotation of cane and any other crop does not make an even rotation or alternation. The corn made fine mule feed, and some planters put in about an acre of corn for each acre of cane planted. Peas, and in later years, soybeans were planted in the corn, and these leguminous crops helped to replenish the fertility of the soil. With the passing of the mule, there is more feed for cattle in the cane country.

Sugar country has always had much about it that was attractive. Growing cane and corn make beautiful landscapes throughout spring, summer, and fall. Old plantation houses still display the quality and style of architecture of the planters' most prosperous period. Although there is a popular misconception as to the number of houses of classical quality in the South, the sugar cane country of the southeastern part of the prairies, especially along the bayous, affords many fine examples of interesting architecture. They vary in style, having been built by architects from various areas. They usually are not the product of true Acadian country.

11

The Cotton
and Corn Country

THE cotton and corn country of southwest Louisiana developed in old cattle country, and it became quite distinctively old Cajun country. It is in the old cotton and corn country that most of these sketches had their origin. It was less spectacular than the cane country, but therein lies its interest.

Just as De Boré's discovery started the sugar industry on its way, so did the invention of the cotton gin by Eli Whitney start cotton production on its way. The gin was invented in 1793, and that date marks the beginning of expansion of cotton production in the south. In southwest Louisiana, cotton country lies generally just to the east and northeast of the cane country. It was the country of the *petit habitant,* and it was country in which families supplied most of their own labor.

It took until perhaps 1880 for cotton to get fully established in its particular region, and from then on there was little change in its boundaries. Cotton production moved westward across the Acadian prairies as far as the land was deemed good enough and well-drained enough, and there it stopped. Land not right for cotton was left in pasture or grazing, and most of that was later plowed up for rice planting. Thus the cotton country appears on a map between the cane country on the east and the rice country on the west.

For a long time this country changed but slowly. A farmer put perhaps 40 per cent of his land in cotton and 40 per cent in corn. The next year he alternated those two patches, so the rotation was a simple one. The rest of his land he used for minor crops, vegetables, and pasture. In recent decades sweet potatoes, dairying, vegetable raising, and a few other commercial activities have altered this picture. Replacement of many mules by tractors and mechanization has been a part of the modern trend. As indicated previously several times, these sketches are concerned more strongly with the development of the prairies over the long period rather than the most recent times, so let us see what took place in the occupation and settlement of the cotton country and how the people lived in the subsequent decades.

First, one should recall the invention of the cotton gin (1793) and the coming of the steam packet to the streams of Attakapas and Opelousas about 1812. There had been some competition between cane and cotton for land, and the lower Têche went primarily to sugar cane. The upper Têche, the streams in the vicinity of Opelousas, and some of the bluff lands went in for cotton. Old newspapers told of the hauling of 750 bales of cotton from Vermilionville (now Lafayette) to the Têche in 1825. Major Amos Stoddard, in his *Sketches, Historical and Descriptive, of Louisiana,* told in 1812 of cotton being produced in the Opelousas country: "This scene [Opelousas prairie country] is diversified by the houses and plantations scattered along the edges of the woods. Cotton and cattle are at present the staple commodities of this district; but the inhabitants are about to direct their attention to the culture of sugar cane which is much more profitable. This has been hitherto delayed for want of capital to carry it on."

The indications from several sources are that in the better alluvial and bluff lands near Opelousas, there was a strong tendency and attraction toward the production of sugar. Smaller farmers and those who lacked capital went into cotton. However, in that section there were many planters who produced cotton under the plantation system with Negro slave labor.

An Opelousas newspaper of 1866 told of fine crops of corn and cotton on the prairies seven miles west of Opelousas and at Prud'homme City still farther west. The *Opelousas Journal* of March 28, 1868, printed a lengthy sketch by one of its reporters who had just taken a ride over that country. Here is a part of it: "Leaving the town of Opelousas and turning our faces toward the setting sun, we pass a beautiful rolling prairie country. . . . On every hand we beheld farms plowed up and already planted in corn and cotton, with here and there a small quantity of cane."

The *Opelousas Courier* of March 9, 1878, said that in the previous year the town of Washington shipped 30,000 bales of cotton and 32,000 sacks of cotton seed. The same year 3,000 hogsheads of sugar and 5,800 barrels of molasses were shipped by packet from that port, which is about six miles from Opelousas. From the newspapers and the many agricultural notices, it was evident that the cotton in the Opelousas country came from the prairie areas and the sugar cane from the alluvial lowlands, particularly on Bayous Boeuf and Courtableau.

In 1884 Eugene W. Hilgard said in the *Report of Cotton Production in the United States,* Part I, that "the Cote Gelee, Vermilion, Grand Coteau, and Opelousas Prairies, when reasonably well cultivated, produce from 1,000 to 1,200 pounds of seed-cotton per acre, the staple rating as fair middling. Cotton is by far the most prominent culture. Corn is produced for home consumption, only yielding 20 to 40 bushels per acre. Cultivation is generally shallow, and doubtless for that reason the actual cotton product per acre has greatly decreased in the older districts."

Natural increase in the Acadian population helped to fill up the cotton country and caused the holdings to be cut into smaller and smaller tracts. The larger bayou front grants which had been used as *vacheries* were cut lengthwise into many strips, and even the strips were cut in transverse fashion. Some of these are seen on Bayou Vermilion. Although farmers, for a time, cultivated only a few acres of the highest land on their homesteads, with better drainage and pressure upon the land, they have long since cultivated it all. Land-utilization maps and aerial photographs show that practically all of the land in the whole cotton and corn section is under cultivation or improved.

Under the rectangular land pattern of the United States Land Office, section lines were laid out and space for roads was left between the sections which, of course, were one mile square. For a long time no attempt was made at building or improving the so-called "public roads," but after a time farmers began to grade or work them. As there were no building materials such as stone, gravel, or shells available, those roads remained as gumbo dirt roads with terribly poor drainage. "Muddy when wet and dusty when dry" is really an understatement as applied to those roads. It does not convey at all how bad they really were. Now the country roads have been improved nearly everywhere with better drainage and gravel, and the through roads are surfaced as modern concrete and blacktop roads.

Drainage used to be the main problem. The early settlers had picked the high spots—often these were natural levees of streams which have long since shifted their courses elsewhere. One of the least kind things a neighbor could say about a farm was: "You would have a nice place here if it weren't so low." That remark evoked a sense of injury not soon forgotten.

Low lands, formerly called "flats" (such as the Foreman Flat

near Duson and Marais Bullard), were considered absolutely un-
fit for cultivation before World War I. Now they are drained
and fully utilized. Older houses, by their distribution, often mark
out the high land. There once was not so much need for putting
one's house by the side of the road; the farmer just put it on his
highest land. With the improvement of roads and the modern
inclination to be located near the surfaced road, some farmers
moved their houses to roadside locations. Others who felt the
need for newer and more modern houses have, in many cases,
located their new houses on roadside sites. Thus we see changing
patterns even in an area of exceedingly slight change generally.

The small farmer was really a small farmer, from the modern
point of view. One old-timer said that "a crop of two bales of cotton was too small; a crop of four bales was too much work; a
crop of three bales was 'just right.'" With improved tools, more
knowledge about cultivation, better varieties of cotton and insecticides, the production of a single farmer has gone steadily up-
ward. Limitation by government control of course held down
acreage at times since the thirties, but with the cut in acreage
came better methods of production. Through the use of better
seed, better tillage, and fertilizer and insecticides, a cut in acreage
means little other than the fact that it permits land to be turned
to other uses. Whereas half a bale to the acre once was good

TYPE OF HOUSE occupied by an Acadian sharecropper. His wife kept her
little chickens in the coops shown in the foreground. (Photograph tak-
en in 1935.)

WARREN ARCENEAUX, a farmer in Acadia Parish, returns from his field with a small pair of cotton mules and a walking plow. Note the type of harness used on the cotton farms. (Photograph taken in 1935.)

enough, now farmers aim to pick as high as two bales to the acre. And this increased yield is on the very same land that the modern farmer's grandfather cropped.

The farmstead of the cotton farmer was anything but pretentious. As those people farmed only small tracts averaging perhaps forty acres in size, incomes were small and levels of living correspondingly low. A dwelling in the cotton country was as different from the mansion of the cane country as a Creole cotton mule was from a Missouri-bred sugar mule. Barns and outbuildings were still more inexpensive in appearance, and as to some of the poorer share croppers' houses, the less said the better. Some of them had only two rooms, no porches, and about them there were no shade trees.

Inclosures included a pasture of a few acres, a small pig pen, a garden, and a lot or pen for the mules. There may have been a small yard in front of the house, but by and large, little was wasted on the poorer share cropper homes.

Sweet potatoes have always been a significant part of the subsistence of the Acadian family. Each farmer planted a few rows of sweet potatoes as early as possible so that they would make vines for the main planting. After he dug his Irish potatoes, when the June and July rains were on, he planted his sweet potato vines in his specially prepared patch. Even though the quality of the potatoes for a long time was not good, yields have always been great, and each fall the farmer stored an ample supply of potatoes for later use. One way of storing them was outside in a hill or "butte." The farmer would merely put a big pile of potatoes in a little pen back of his house and cover it with straw. Then he covered the whole thing with dirt and topped it with an inverted tin tub. This was part of his family's food supply for the winter and spring, and on warm days during the winter he would open one side of the butte and take out a barrel or so of potatoes for immediate use. Then he would cover the hole. Toward spring, he cleaned up the pile and put the remaining potatoes in his barn. That was the old way of handling sweet potatoes.

Now sweet potato production has gone commercial. The higher, well-drained lands of sandier quality, in an area generally bounded by Lafayette, Carencro, Sunset, Opelousas, Church Point and Rayne, are some of the most important areas of commercial production of potatoes in the whole country. Again, improved varieties and quality of product have helped to make the industry a successful one. Proper grading of product as to size and quality is required, and facilities for handling and storage have developed as needed. The Yambilee, or yam celebration, in Opelousas is expressive of the importance placed upon this industry, which is located in what used to be cotton and corn country.

Subsistence production played an important part in the lives of the people. "He lives at home" was an expression meaning that a man raised almost everything he ate. Long ago they began canning and preserving fruits, vegetables, and meats, and it was with great pride that a housewife showed you her pantry with perhaps five hundred or a thousand jars and cans of food available for use at any time. Indeed, they "lived at home."

In addition to the sweet potatoes there were, of course, Irish potatoes produced as needed and perhaps for sale. A row of okra was a landmark of an Acadian home. This product the housewife usually fried, but okra was used also in making okra gumbo, a favorite dish. Alongside the row of okra was always a row, or perhaps a double row, of butter beans. These beans furnished a fresh food all summer long, and in the fall the remaining dry beans were picked and stored for winter use.

A row or two of tomatoes, a few rows of watermelons, and other vegetables not well suited for growing in the small garden were always planted in the field, usually near the gate.

Popcorn, peanuts, and *benne* (sesame) were also planted and used for making pralines. Obviously, some of those old-timers not only "lived at home," but they lived very well.

12

The Rice
and Cattle Country

THE rice country of southwest Louisiana is really rice and cattle country, because after years of experimentation the rice farmers settled down to rotation or alternation in the use of the land. This area consists of that portion of the prairies not previously taken up by the sugar cane and corn country or the cotton and corn country described in the two previous sketches. This whole landscape presents a checkerboard of changing landscapes. The rice fields themselves change colors several times during the year and, of course, the fields are always different from the land that is being grazed.

The rice country is, in a way, an outlier of the grain belt of the Middle West. It was settled by wheat farmers who had used machinery to produce a grain that was sold commercially. They merely applied wheat machinery to the cultivation of rice. It was in this respect that the American farmers were different from their Acadian predecessors on the prairies.

Previously, rice had been produced mainly in low places, such as the lowlands of South Carolina and on the natural levees of the Mississippi River, but nowhere was it raised on a field culture plan like that developed farther north in the raising of wheat. The old Acadians followed a sort of oriental system of hand culture in the raising of rice—they planted it in places that one could have scarcely plowed. They planted it in the *coulées* and ponds, and in that humid climate flooding it was no problem at all. When it was ripe they cut it with sickles and threshed it by hand. Then they hulled it in the Oriental style with the wooden mortar and pestle. No part of Acadian rice growing was on a large scale.

One of the most significant developments to come out of the small scale rice industry, however, was the eating of rice. Those old French people, as well as the Spanish people, learned to cook rice and to eat rice. They made it such an important part of their diet in soups, gumbos, and jambalayas that no meal was complete without it.

After 1880 and the completion of the Southern Pacific Railroad, the central and western parts of the Acadian prairies were made known to outsiders. From then on, a large part of the story has to do with Anglo-Saxon people. The outsiders, skilled in the ways of advertising, promoting real estate sales, transportation, large-scale wheat farming, and engineering problems, took the lead and promoted large-scale rice growing and mechanization of the agriculture and milling phases of the industry.

Not only was the industry unique in the above-mentioned ways, but the promoters of the industry visualized a type of agriculture in which white men would do most of the work—a departure from a generally established custom in the South. As time passed, other people besides the original English-speaking rice farmers moved in. Acadians moved in, and at the eastern fringe of the rice country some of them shifted or alternated between the growing of rice and cotton. Some actual French settlers from France came in and established themselves as important rice farm-

Characteristic rice harvesting scene in Acadia Parish before World War I. This self-binding reaper is drawn by seven mules with four leaders and three on the tongue. This was the customary hitch until mules were replaced by tractors. (Photograph by the late Whitfield D. Post, about 1912.)

ers in Acadia Parish. Germans came in and occupied Robert's Cove and Faquetaïque; in time they became rice farmers on a large scale. Negro laborers moved in also and found employment in the rice mills, warehouses, and at many of the jobs connected with rice growing, hauling, and shipping. The result is that after about three-quarters of a century the rice country has quite a mixed population. With education, and especially with the movement of country people to the towns and cities, the mixing is further complicated. The penetration of oil field workers has brought still greater complexity to the country which the early promoters had visualized as an area to be occupied by ambitious and energetic rice farmers.

As might be expected, the rice boom was led by certain individuals of foresight, ambition, and energy. The open country, with cheap land and a new railroad, presented just the right type of challenge to the promoter and financier. The railroad and other interests tended to bring the same results—immigrants to settle the prairies and begin growing rice.

Seaman A. Knapp was an educator, agriculturalist, and traveler. He had traveled in the Orient and studied rice growing there. He brought back a greatly superior variety of Japanese seed rice and, through his continued efforts and teaching, helped in getting the new type of rice growing established. W. W. Duson and many others made contributions to the industry. Each step seemed to call for some new development or adaptation, but there was always sufficient ingenuity and skill present to solve any of the problems.

One of the more significant problems was met by nature herself. Whereas the bottomless flats of South Carolina and the alluvial lands on the banks of the Mississippi River had not permitted the use of heavy machinery, the prairies were underlaid by a type of claypan locally called "hardpan" which made possible the use of heavy machines and, later, tractors and combines. Not only did the claypan help in that way, but it helped to conserve water, as it is practically impervious to the downward seepage of water. The claypan and the flatness of the land made the flooding of rice a simple operation. The water supply for irrigating was greatly increased by the drilling of semi-artesian wells several hundred feet deep. First these wells were pumped by steam

RICE IN THE SHOCK in Acadia Parish in 1934. Much rice is now harvested with combines, so shocking is not necessary.

power and later by diesel power. Today one sees water for irrigation being pumped both from the local streams and from the wells.

Gangplows, disks, cutaways, harrows, seeders, drills, self-binding reapers, and threshing machines were all put to use. All of these were first drawn by mules, most of which were brought in from elsewhere, but in time they were replaced by tractors. Rice raising on the old Acadian prairies is now about as highly mechanized as any agricultural industry in the world. Nor does the mechanization stop with production. The transportation and milling problems are handled in equivalent fashion and on a grand scale.

Throughout the rice country there are landmarks of the works of the pioneers, but one may see changes taking place. Black Angus cattle are seen by the thousands grazing the rice land in its off years, and so important are the cattle that some farmers have revised their system of rotation so as to make use of improved grasses, on a less temporary basis. Commercial fertilizers are used, as are the very best seeds available.

Whether Acadians make up more than half of the population of the rice country today would be difficult to say, but certainly, in some areas they are in majority. One may hear Acadian-French spoken on the streets of any of the rice land towns, and one's doctor, dentist, lawyer, or teacher in Acadia or Calcasieu parish is very apt to be an Acadian.

13

Cajun Houses

W E used to call Ca-
jun houses "old timey houses." They were the oldest houses that
we knew, and we could tell them from about a mile away. From
a distance the distinctive features in a Cajun house are the built-in
porch and the high steep-pitched roof.

Other people called them "daubed houses" because their walls
were daubed on the inside with mud and Spanish moss or *barbe
espagnole*. Others would have called them "half-timbered houses."
Whereas the French-speaking people over on the Mississippi River
sometimes filled their wall spaces from the inside with loose
bricks, the prairie Acadians used the local mud for that purpose.

Throughout the prairies, as elsewhere in French-speaking Louisiana, sawed lumber was always used in building houses. Those
people never built log houses. There were no logs suitable for
building on the prairies, of course, but even near the woods, where

such logs might possibly have been found, the Acadians invariably sawed all small lumber for their houses.

All Cajun houses had the built-in porch. It is an integral part of the house, as it is under the main rafters which form a great symmetrical inverted "V" with a gable at each end. Of course the porch, which runs the full length of the house, is at the front side, the side toward the road. The advantages of the steep roof were two-fold. It shed water better, and it also made a spacious attic that could house a loom and also furnish a sleeping room for some of the boys.

Oddly enough, the Cajun house is wider than it is long, the length being the distance from gable to gable. Such houses are usually about twenty-four feet long and thirty-six feet wide. That of course, is the main part of the house. The kitchen, or kitchen and dining room combined, was sometimes added at a later date and as an appendage to the main structure. In such cases the kitchen formed a "T" or an "L." In other cases the kitchen was added at the end of the house as an extension. Somehow, the

OLD GUIDRY HOUSE near Rayne, in 1935. It has since burned down. Note the built-in porch, the stairs leading to the attic. The walls of this house were daubed with mud and Spanish moss. The yard or flower garden is characteristic.

OLD ACADIAN HOUSE with a false gallery. The stairs on the front porch are characteristic, as are the combination dining room and kitchen at the end of the main structure.

extension never seems to fit. If the front side of the kitchen was even with the front wall, the roof and backside didn't fit, and vice-versa. But there is a distinct advantage to putting the kitchen at the end of the house. It permitted the housewife to see who was passing in the road at the front.

The heavier timbers of those houses usually were hand-hewn, and all of the main joints of the older ones were mortised and then secured with wooden pegs. Originally the roofs were made of shakes; many of these were later replaced by shingles; and now a great many of the houses are under a third roof, usually sheet metal.

Daubing the walls of a house was an important process, as the mud was said to have made houses "warm in winter and cool in summer." When a house was ready to be daubed, a big hole was dug in the yard. Into it went mud, moss, and water. These were tramped and stirred until the consistency was right, and then the mixture was daubed into the spaces between the studs. Usually this space was about four inches in thickness. After the walls were sufficiently dry, they were trimmed off smoothly with a sharp spade. Then the inside walls were whitewashed.

The front wall of the house was protected by the porch, so in some houses that wall was not boarded in. From the front, one could see the studs and the daubing. The other three sides of the house which were not protected from the weather, however, were always weather-boarded. House after house in other parts of French-speaking Louisiana show this feature, but it seems to have been somewhat less common on the prairies.

The adding of a kitchen was one way of making a house bigger, but there were still other ways. One was to just move two houses together, end to end. In such cases the chimney was usually a double one right at the junction, so that two rooms had the benefit of fireplaces. Several houses near the Plaquemine Brulée woods were made in this way. On the prairies a few houses were made by putting one house in front of another. This made the roofs look like an inverted "W," or a cockscomb. This system was more common east of the Mississippi, especially at French Settlement.

Nowadays it is difficult to find a mud chimney, but long ago that was the common type. They have since been replaced by brick chimneys. The mud chimney was made with four poles, the cross sticks to hold the mud. These were then given a generous daubing of mud and Spanish moss. The job was a smooth one, and often was the result of a day's work by a "mud party." This was a sort of co-operative institution, or daubing bee. Some houses had the chimney at one end, some had a chimney at each end, and still others had the double chimney at the center.

The feature which probably has drawn the most comment from outsiders is the stairway located on the front porch of the older houses—it leads up to the attic. House after house shows this feature. If one should find an old Cajun house not having the stairs on the front porch, inquiry would soon show that the stairs had been removed. These stairs vary widely in their construction. Some are almost as simple as ladders, and they go straight up in one single flight. Others are much more elaborate and have one turn in them near the floor. Some of these even have lockers built under them. One reason for placing the stairs on the porch is to allow more space inside. Also, stairs always furnish a few more seats on the porch when a big crowd gathers.

The *fausse galerie,* or false gallery, is an extension of the porch roof or, more properly, a visor which helps protect the porch from sun and rain. On the prairies, the few false galleries that one sees are all shingled, but east of the Mississippi they seem to be made invariably of boards resembling shakes. The false gallery is much more common in the northern section of the prairies than the southern, and the feature dies out completely well north of the Southern Pacific Railroad line.

A single railing once adorned most front porches of Cajun houses. This railing usually was a 2″ x 4″ timber set about three feet above the floor, running from post to post, to serve at least two purposes. One was to keep people from falling off the porch and the other was to afford something to sit on and lean on.

Front doors are double and swing out. A rather small house has one, but usually there are two. Of the two it frequently is impossible to tell which leads into the "front room." This is especially true where there are two sets of steps to the front porch.

Most of the older houses at one time had wooden shutters for windows, but some of them have been replaced by glass windows. Only the poorest houses still have the wooden shutters, but they are not hard to find. Occasionally one sees houses with glass windows to the main rooms, and wooden shutters for the attic windows. Heavy hand-wrought hooks were used to fasten both doors and windows in very old Cajun houses, but many of these have been replaced by store-bought catches.

The old houses have no closets whatsoever. It was expected that the lady of the house would bring in an *armoire* or two with

A POT SHELF or *tablette* outside the window of an Acadian house. This one was built as a museum piece at the Acadian Craft Shop in Longfellow State Park at St. Martinville.

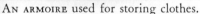

AN ARMOIRE used for storing clothes.

the rest of her furniture, and these would serve as clothes closets. Similarly, in the kitchen there were no built-in cabinets. There was a tall *garde-manger,* or screened "safe," which housed kitchenware and kept the flies off the food. The *tablette,* or pot shelf, is an interesting feature of Acadian homes. It is a small wooden shelf built outside the kitchen window sill and flush with it. With a pot shelf one can stand inside the kitchen and wash dishes outside. When the dishes are finished, the water is just thrown out the window—sometimes into a mudhole. This shelf is quite convenient for used pots or for setting out hot dishes to cool. On the prairies, where the potshelf was not very common, it was never housed in, but farther east, on some of the bayous, the shelf was housed in on both ends and at the top so as to have protection from the weather.

House painting in Acadian country developed some peculiar characteristics. In the first place, paint was not thought of as a preservative of wood and lumber. It was just an expensive way of beautifying a house. Whitewashing was something else. It was a cheap and rustic way of accomplishing the same purpose. Consider the dilemma of the people who were "too poor to paint and too proud to whitewash"!

Since the front wall was so often a bare mud wall, the thing to do was to whitewash the wall and let the other three go unpainted. Besides, the whitewash lasted better under the protection of the porch. Out of this apparently came the custom of painting only the front wall. In driving along some country roads, one may see house after house with only the front wall painted. This applies as well to the newer frame houses. Another time one may drive along a different road, where the houses are completely painted. People tend to do as their neighbors do, and the same applies to the colors used in painting the trimming. Windows and doors get coats of green, blue, red, or various other colors, and sometimes for miles on end every house will have the same color trimming. The houses left unpainted are weathered into a soft gray which is eventually appliquéd, here and there, by dull green, gold, and gray mosses and lichen.

House hauling was a peculiar custom which apparently was quite widely followed in some sections of the prairies. Some of the houses were completely built (*tout fait*) over on the Mermen-

A DOUBLE ACADIAN HOUSE with two fireplaces, the characteristic steep-pitched roof, built-in porch, and stairs on the front porch. The front yard is fenced in with chicken wire; the chinaberry tree was topped earlier during the year.

tau River where there were saw mills, and they were hauled across the prairies to their present sites. Joseph Moore, an old Acadian living in Mermentau back in 1934, said that when he was young he built more than a dozen of them and sold them to settlers who hauled them to their tracts, sometimes thirty-five or forty miles away.

When a man bought a house in Mermentau, he called his neighbors together and organized a hauling bee, or *halerie*. With a dozen yoke of oxen and three wagons they soon had the house underway with no difficulty. First they took the beds off two wagons, and in place of the regular coupling poles they used long logs perhaps thirty feet long. They jacked up the house, then ran the poles under it. Next they chained them up to the two front pair of wheels, thus supporting the house, and it was ready to roll. They hitched five or six yoke of oxen to each of the wagons, and away they went across the open prairie. With no fields, ditches, or fences to hinder them, they could make twelve or fifteen miles per day. As they could live in the house while it was being moved, house hauling was very easy; it was the easiest way to solve the housing problem at that time.

As Cajun houses were not aristocratic houses—so many of them were built by the people themselves rather than by professional architects—they have received little attention. Their origin is really not very clear, although half-timbered houses are common in France. There the people use bricks and stone rather than clay for filling in the walls. The porch is different however, in the New World. It may have come from the West Indies.

H. M. Brackenridge, who traveled through Louisiana in 1811, described houses and settlements for various places as far north as Kaskaskia. He wrote in his *View of Louisiana with a Journal up the Missouri River in 1811,* of the "creole house" in Kaskaskia, giving the main features of the Acadian type of house. He said that it was reported to have come from the West Indies. It is still found throughout French Louisiana, with variations, but always with the built-in porch. It might be noted here that in some cases, the built-in porch has been closed to make additional rooms, but it cannot be concealed or disguised completely.

Probably no Cajun house has been built on the prairies in the past fifty years. They have been superseded by more modern houses with bungalows being among the most numerous types. But they should not be counted out yet. Some of them are still in use, and a few will be occupied on the prairies for many years to come. A few have been set aside as museums, a notable case being the one in Longfellow State Park in St. Martinville. It has many of the features commonly found in the true Cajun house.

Immediately in front of the old Acadian house there was a small yard, an inclosure within an inclosure. The larger inclosure was really a small pasture for the calves, the family horse, and perhaps a pair of work mules. The smaller one would have been considered by most people merely a flower garden, for that is what it usually was. From the little swinging gate to the front steps of the house ran a walk bordered by low flowers such as violets, and in some cases two rows of bottles with their necks stuck into the ground served the same purpose.

But the distinguishing features of the front yard were two big cape jasmine plants, one on each side of the walk. They not only dominated the floral scene, but they perfumed the air both day and night in spring and summer. Red cannas, rose bushes, four o'clocks, zinnias, and marigolds all had their seasons, but it was the jasmine that gave the scene the Acadian accent.

In the old days the garden fence may have been of horizontal *pieux,* but to make a fence that would keep out the chickens, the housewife usually saw to it that a stockade fence was made with cypress posts set vertically and quite close together. Where security was not so essential, a board fence about four boards high sufficed. In later years, chicken wire and the other patented wire fences replaced the older styles. The newer fences met all of the requirements, and besides, they showed a progressive tendency.

14

Cajun Pieu Fences

In the old days, before nails and barbed wire were available for fence building, the Cajuns built a type of rail-and-post fence with broad split rails which they called *pieux*. They were quite different in construction from the Anglo-Saxon zig-zag, or Lincoln fence, which was characteristic of north Louisiana.

The *pieux* were split rails somewhat pointed at each end so as to fit into holes in the properly spaced vertical posts. The chief labor in the building of such a fence was the boring and cutting of holes in the uprights. After that was done, building the fence proceeded at a rapid rate. The fence was pleasing to look at, it held hogs and sheep as well as cattle and horses, and it did not necessarily involve an outlay of cash, as no nails were needed in its construction. The old *Opelousas Journal,* on March 8, 1872, published the cost of building fences with *pieux*. It also described the construction:

Nine foot pieux cost now at Washington [six miles from Opelousas] twelve dollars per hundred, and the hauling to Opelousas three dollars. Sixteen panels of fence would take seventeen pieux for posts; the remaining 83 would make 16 panels, five pieux to each panel, and having three left. Deducting six inches from each pieux for tenons, make an aggregate of 8 feet, the sixteen panels of fence would be 136 feet long or a little less than 45 yards. The cost of building the fence is 25 cents per panel, or $4, for the 16 panels. The total cost of a pieux fence 45 yards in length at Opelousas is $19. This makes $1.18 to the panel, 42 and a fraction cents per yard and 14 cents and a fraction to the foot.

Although this cost seems outrageously high, most *pieux* were not bought for cash but were taken in trade. In the old days they were procured at Washington (to which point they were brought on Bayou Courtableau) and at Mermentau, on the river of the same name, as well as at various other streams where cypress was available. From the streams they were hauled on wagons and oxcarts across the prairie to be sold or traded for corn or cattle.

AN ACADIAN FENCE five *pieux* high. Whereas there used to be hundreds of miles of such fences on the prairies, they are great rarities today. Gaston Moore had some old *pieux,* and he rebuilt this fence just to oblige the photographer. (June, 1935.)

On top of the load it was not at all unusual to see a wooden dugout hog trough, or a mortar, or perhaps a few ox-yokes. These were articles usually carried to trade off to the farmers.

According to several old residents of the Cajun country, all fences were made of *pieux* until about 1890. After that, boards and barbed wire came into use. On country roads as late as the 1930's one could occasionally see a bit of *pieu* fence, but one was much more apt to see some of the old *pieux* nailed to the fence posts in a more modern fashion. Their tenons had rotted off, but the sound portions of the *pieux* were nailed to the posts just as one nails boards to posts in building a board fence. Old *pieux* were to be seen in the Atchafalaya Basin or almost anywhere on the prairies, but to most current residents they would never be recognized for what they had been, for few living residents of the Acadian prairies have ever seen a real *pieu* fence, except perhaps on a dude ranch.

Considerable labor was involved in making the *pieux* and in building the fences, but some settlers took great pride in them and even fenced in all their land. A pasture fence was built "four *pieux* high" and was usually on top of a little ridge which was accentuated by two small ditches on either side of the ridge.

Each stockman had at least a pen or small pasture for his milk stock, in the use of which great economy was practiced. The calves of the milk cows were kept in the pen during the day while the cows were allowed to graze on the open prairies. At night, after milking, the cows were kept penned up and the calves were allowed to run loose. The system was quite practical in view of the old Acadian method of milking, in which the presence of the calf at milking time is about as important as the presence of the cow herself.

As fields were small and the prairie large, the fences stood out on the landscape. If the field was irregular in shape because of the necessity for including only the crowns of natural levees, they curved to follow the contour. Those ridges, which even on the prairies were called *coteaux,* naturally were the first areas fenced in. When the field was changed, moving the fence was a simple matter, and some share tenants in the last quarter of the last century even had *pieux* which they moved from place to place.

The fencing in of eighty or a hundred acres with *pieux* was not entirely unusual, and some settlers fenced in even more land. But the enclosing of the yard around the house and the small pens with *pieux* was by far the most common practice. The use made of the "rails" in Pine Prairie by one settler is shown in a claim made late in the eighteenth century: "John McDaniel, before the Board on the 10th of February, 1812, hath deposed 'that about fourteen years ago there was a cabin built, and about sixteen hundred rails split and used in enclosing cow-pens, and some small fields' which were put in cultivation by the deponent who continued to reside thereon . . . "[1] Whether McDaniel meant rails or *pieux* one cannot say, but the use he made of his fences was the same as that made by other men with *pieux* fences. In 1870 Lockett made the following observation of an industrious Negro homesteader who lived at the edge of Prairie Mamou:

> They (Pierre Noir and his family) had come to the western border of Prairie Mamou since the war and settled in a point of woods that projected into the prairie like a cape into the sea. Pierre *entered* the land upon which he settled and closed with fences several hundred acres of woodland and prairie, and divided his domain into lots of about forty acres area each . . . . His horses and cattle run upon the common prairie during the grass season, but they are regularly driven into one of the lots for salting at stated intervals. In another the cows with young calves and the mares with colts are kept, and all the herds are kept under fence during the winter and fed. In this way one half of the farm is tramped and thoroughly manured, and put in fine condition for receiving a crop the next season.[2]

Pierre's use of his fences was admirable, but Lockett went on

[1]*American State Papers,* Public Lands, III, 100.
[2]Samuel Henry Lockett, *Louisiana As It Is: A Geographical and Topographical Description of the State . . . 1873* (Manuscript, Tulane University Library, New Orleans, La.), 51.

to say that it was in marked contrast to the practices of most of the Creoles in the prairies. He was passing through, at that time, one of the poorer sections of the prairies. It is very evident today that the people in many sections of the prairies fared better than the ones which Lockett described.

Undoubtedly the unique case of fencing was the enclosing in Acadia Parish of the William Wikoff grant of slightly more than five thousand acres with *pieux* (see page 93). One present owner of a tract of land within the original grant pointed out the little levee which surrounded the grant and upon which the fence was built. He said that the levee was about two feet high at the crest and about five feet wide at the base. The ditches on each side were a couple of feet wide, making the fence, levee, and ditches quite a formidable barrier. The work was done by Irishmen who worked by contract, and they took years to build it, but the fence stood for a long time. During the Civil War, when the men were away, the *pieux* were a wood supply to housewives of the neighborhood. Today some old *pieux* can be seen on the place, and only the slightest trace of the levee and ditches remain. Other fences and graded and dredged ditches present a far more complex pattern, but still, as a single endeavor, nothing on the place matches the magnitude of the task of making that levee and fence.

Another type of fence was built of vertical *pieux* or pickets. They are still in common use for yards and gardens. Of course, nails are used in each picket nowadays but, formerly, they were held in place, at least partly, by horizontal strips nailed across them. Sometimes a picket was left unnailed so that it could be temporarily removed to permit one to pass through the fence. Such a loose picket was and still is called a *passe pieu*.

The yard, which is a small inclosure often within a larger pasture, still involves fencing, as does a small garden which is apart from the yard. The yard fence is never moved, but occasionally the garden site is changed. In so doing the fence is taken down in sections and moved to the new location.

Barbed wire is now used in fencing almost all pastures for cattle and horses, but hog wire and boards are used in building fences that are supposed to hold hogs and small calves. Formerly, no one ever attempted to keep chickens penned up, but in that matter times have changed.

Old hedges of Cherokee rose are still to be seen here and there along section roads. Some of them were planted to serve as fences, and others were planted to serve as windbreaks. Probably their present owners regret that they were ever planted, as they take up considerable space and are difficult to eradicate when not wanted.

In the old days the stock laws were largely a matter of local option. Some parishes required that the fields be fenced by their owners, and others required that cattle be kept penned or, at least, off the road. Acadia Parish permitted stock to run loose; it was the responsibility of the farmer to fence in his fields. Lafayette Parish did not permit stock to run loose, so many fields were unfenced.

Following All Saints' Day most of the cattle and hogs were turned loose. Gates were opened and the stock were permitted to roam at will. It was a case of the custom being stronger than the law. But modern highways, the automobile, and various other factors have brought into force laws that are stronger than any old custom.

15

Old Aladdin
and His Creole Chairs

As you enter an Acadian house, you are asked to *"prenez une chaise"* or take a chair. In the old days such a chair would undoubtedly have been what was commonly called a "creole chair" which was a straight-backed chair with a cowhide seat. Most notable probably was the fact that the hair was still on the hide. A red-and-white or black-and-white hide made the prettier chair seats. This was the kind of creole chair that old Aladdin sold for a dollar each.

Aladdin lived by the woods, and all summer long he worked at his trade. Then in the fall he piled his wagon high with chairs and started across the prairie selling them to any farmer who would buy them. He always asked for cash in his dealings, but in hard times he would take almost anything in trade, such as corn, chickens, and even little pigs. Before he got home he always had a motley collection of supplies and livestock.

THE LATE JAKE LOCKLEY and some of his creole chairs. He was about the last of the old chair makers in Acadia Parish, and even he had gone in for power tools. Note the hide which is to be used in making chair seats.

The creole chair was entirely a homemade product. It was the product of Aladdin's hands and feet; for with his hands he worked with saws, augurs, drawing knives, and manipulated the lathe which he actually turned by foot power. His materials were as simple as his tools. With a few slabs of ash, hickory, red gum, and green unsalted hides, he was ready to start work.

The posts of straight backed chairs were made of green ash turned down on the lathe to about two inches in diameter; the chair backs were made of red gum; and the rungs were of dry hickory. When assembled and allowed to dry, the green wood set on the dry wood making a snug fit of neat workmanship without the use of any glue or nails in the entire chair. The seat was put on and laced underneath so that when dry it was always smooth and tight.

Few creole chairs were ever painted. The Acadian women scrubbed them with soap or lye and made them very light and neat in appearance. One old chairmaker said that some people wanted solid colors in the seats because they lasted longer. In the creole chairs they got a product that would last through half a century of constant use.

After 1910 Aladdin quit making chairs as did most of the other old chairmakers. An exception was the late Jake Lockley of Rayne who continued making chairs until well into the thirties. He even installed a power lathe instead of the old foot-lathe, and also made rocking chairs. The straight-backed creole chair is still used in Acadian homes.

16

Spinning and Weaving

MANY a Cajun boy was still wearing *cotonnade* (homespun cotton) trousers, dyed a light blue, long after the turn of the century, and a number of homespun articles such as blankets and bedspreads outlasted the trousers. In the thirties spinners and weavers were rare. By then most of the old handlooms had been chopped up for kindling. One of the best known weavers then was the late Madame Ophé Benoit, who was still active until about ten years ago. She and her daughter, Adolphina, lived about eight miles northwest of Lafayette and four miles west of Carencro. They worked together for many years with the wheel and loom making bedspreads, tablecloths, napkins, and rugs. Adolphina still weaves, but her other activities keep her quite busy most of the time. Weavers are indeed hard to find now, even among the Acadians.

The techniques of spinning and weaving were brought to the

Cajun country with the earliest settlements, and they seem to have remained unchanged. The wheels all appeared to be factory made. At any rate, they had been purchased from stores. The looms, however, were entirely handmade. They were massive in construction being about six feet high, seven feet long, and about six feet wide. All joints were mortised, and pegs rather than nails were used to hold them together. There was a time when the spinning wheel and the loom were standard equipment in almost every Acadian home, but the loom, being so big and clumsy, was kept either in the attic or in a special shed in the back yard.

A few Acadians raised sheep to furnish wool for blankets and cloth, but cotton was by far the main textile used. Indigo dyes made possible a light blue color for the *cotonnade,* and most Acadians planted a few rows of *coton de Siam* which was a *café au lait* color for the sake of variety.

Judged by modern standards, Acadian weaving would be considered quite crude, but the fact that pride was taken in the work is shown by the following letter, which was written about 143 years ago.

To Wade Hampton

NEW ORLEANS, 18th May 1812

Private

DEAR SIR:

Do me the favor to take in charge the enclosed *packet* which the bearer will deliver to you. It encloses a Cotton Blanket manufactured by a very amiable Lady of the country Attackapas within this Territory. Be so good as to present this Blanket in my name to Mrs. [James] Madison, accompanied with the assurances of my great respect, and best wishes for her health and happiness.

I sincerely wish you an agreeable voyage and much prosperity in life.

I am, Sir,

(Signed) W. C. C. CLAIBORNE[1]

[1]Dunbar Rowland (ed.), *Official Letter Books of W. C. C. Claiborne, 1801-1816* (Jackson, Miss., 1917), VI, 100.

THE LATE MADAME BENOIT and her spinning wheel. She bought the wheel at a store when she was married in about 1890. Her daughter Adolphina is about the only Acadian who still spins and weaves.

One acquainted with Acadian weaving might suppose that the "blanket" which was destined to go to the White House was really a white cotton bedspread of a simple checkerboard design made with slightly coarser threads and with raised tufts that make what is called a "popcorn weave."

Handwoven goods were seldom if ever sold. Wool was sometimes woven on shares, and blankets were traded or given away. One Acadian lady who was born in 1870 near Duson made ten blankets and ten bedspreads for each of her three children and a few for herself. Then they chopped up the loom.

The durability of the homespun fabrics is evident from the way they stood up under the beatings they took from the *battoir*, or battling stick, when they were washed. A common scene on Saturday or Monday was that of an Acadian woman at the edge of a bayou behind the house squatting on a board at the water level washing clothes. She invariably was barefoot and had her skirt tucked under her so as not to get it wet. Thus prepared, she splashed and turned the clothes with one hand and used the other to battle them with the *battoir*. The less said about the buttons the better. Soap was used sparingly, but a big iron kettle was used for boiling the clothes before battling them. Nowadays things are quite different. Even a poor sharecropping family today may have an electric washing machine.

MADAME BENOIT at her homemade loom. The Benoits kept their loom busy until World War II; her daughter still uses the loom on occasion.

17

Transportation

W<small>ATER</small> transportation
was never as important in the prairie area as it was in true bayou
country or on the Mississippi. After leaving the Têche and the
Vermilion going west, water transportation was negligible. The
roads followed the natural levees of the bayous to a considerable
extent, and they followed any ridges that may have developed on
the open prairies, but when one had occasion to go visiting across
a prairie, he had to cross five or ten miles of nearly level grassland where there were only cow trails. The Acadians knew the
trails in their own localities, but strangers had difficulty sometimes in "navigating" the prairies. Colonel Lockett used a compass on various occasions in the country west of Opelousas, and
he recommended its use to others: "Through these prairies num-
berless tracks are made by their cattle in their journeys to and
from their watering places which, as previously described, are

HORSES AND BUGGIES at the hitching rack near the church in Duson, Lafayette Parish, May, 1936. There are still a few buggies in use in the vicinity of Duson, Abbeville, Carencro, and Church Point. This area and the Amish country of Pennsylvania are the two main areas in the United States where buggies are still used.

natural ponds, *marais,* and *coulées.* The inhabitants know which of these trails are their 'bon chemins,' but a stranger would do well to rely upon his compass and look sharply to his bearings in traversing these broad spaces so destitute of striking landmarks, as every trail seems equally 'bon' to him."[1] *(Bon chemin* means the right road, not good road.)

The men traveled mostly on horseback. Heavy goods were hauled in oxcarts and wagons, but the vehicle of style used to be the *calèche.* Its construction and use were well described by Thomas C. Nicholls in his "Reminiscences" of 1805 to 1840 from the Teche country. "On Saturday evening, might be seen, caleches, (as they are called) a wooden vehicle, put together with pegs, not a particle of iron being used in their construction, mounted on wheels without tyre, placed on rawhide supporters attached to two little windlasses, behind which they were wound up, to the proper height filled with young ladies and old ladies, wending their way to the coming ball. In the foot of the carriage, might be seen, one or probably two short bags, filled with dollars intended by the old ladies, to furnish the means of indulging in their favorite Game of Vingt-une, during the evening."[2]

Although nothing was more stylish for women than the *calèche* in going to church and to dances, only a few people owned such carriages. They seem to have been restricted mainly to the planter class in the sugar cane country and to the wealthier *vacherie* owners.

The assessment roll for St. Landry Parish for 1846 supposedly listed all of the vehicles in the parish under seven types or head-

[1] Lockett, *Louisiana As It Is,* 48.

[2] Thomas C. Nicholls, "Reminiscences" (copied from the original MS in the possession of Mary Flowers Pugh Russell).

ings and for fifty-two localities. The figures run as follows for the entire parish of St. Landry:

Four-wheeled carriages	90
Two-wheeled carriages	46
Gigs	42
Calèches (mostly two-wheeled)	70
Sulkies	2
Carioles	3
Buggies	2

Men who owned thirty or forty slaves were without wheeled vehicles. Perhaps they simply just forgot to remember them for the assessor.

The thin single-log dugout boat called a pirogue, which is so important on Bayou Lafourche, was scarcely used at all on the prairies. Most notable in the transportation of the Acadians in the first four decades of this century has been the buggy. The horse and buggy has persisted longer in the Amish country of Pennsylvania and the Cajun country of Louisiana than anywhere else in the United States. Even at this writing the buggy is still a feature of rural areas, particularly the cotton and corn section. The hitching racks of all Catholic churches on Sunday mornings until quite recently were all filled to capacity, and on Saturday afternoons buggies frequently caused little traffic snarls all their own. Not only has the buggy held out against the automobile, but some old automobiles have been converted or adapted into horse-drawn vehicles which, if not elegant, still serve useful purposes where people have been long-time holdouts against change. Tenant farmers with their families "go broad" on Sundays in wagons. For years to come we may expect to see some families in their wagons making Sunday trips. For seats they use boards and chairs, neither of which gives a very smooth ride on a rough road, but going broad is fun however one goes.

18

Pile et Pilon:

Mortar and Pestle

"Every time the little dog hears the old woman using the *pile et pilon*, he goes out and catches a chicken." This old Cajun saying means that the little dog was so intelligent, he knew that when the old woman pounded rice with the mortar and pestle they were going to have gumbo and rice for dinner—so he supplied the chicken.

The wooden mortar (*pile,* pronounced peel) was made from a section of log about fifteen or eighteen inches in diameter and about three feet long. The end of the log was hollowed out by burning and chopping for a depth of about six inches, and in this depression corn was cracked and rice was hulled, both by pounding in the Oriental fashion. Some of the old mortars were decorated a bit by working in the outsides of the logs so as to give them wasp waists, a feature often seen in pictures of mortars from Africa and South America.

The pestle (*pilon*) was made from a gum tree pole about four feet long and about four inches in diameter. The middle section of the pestle was worked down so as to be easily grasped with one hand. With these crude implements women cracked corn or hulled rice by the hour. Some of the old Acadians remember when rice was hulled in this fashion, and a few of the very old inhabitants remember when even corn was cracked with the mortar and pestle. Horsepower corn mills supplanted the pestle for grinding corn, and when rice mills came in there was no more use for those hand tools. No one regretted their passing.

Probably no Acadian woman ever stopped to ponder the linguistics associated with her mortar and its products. From the African and Arabic speech of the Negroes came the word *gumbo,* which is a kind of soup made distinctive by the addition of sliced green okra or a bit of sassafras that was pounded in the mortar. And of course, to each dish of gumbo was added a large spoonful of rice—rice that had been hulled in the mortar. If the Acadian wife served corn grits or corn meal mush, she may have called the dish *sacamité, gros gru,* or *couche-couche,* depending upon the extent of the influence of the Indian, French, or African (possibly Arabic) languages. Indian tribes of eastern North America had used various related words from which words like *sacamité* were derived. The English called it *sagamity*—with several different spellings. The French called it *sacamité.* To them it was about the same thing as *gros gru,* or coarse grits. From the Negro slaves introduced into Louisiana were derived the words *gumbo* and *couche-couche,* the latter being a corn cereal, sometimes boiled and sometimes fried, from either grits or corn meal mush. To some, *couche-couche* was just plain corn meal mush.

The Acadians retained a corruption of the Indian word for persimmon. To them, persimmon is *plaquemine,* a fruit honored by both a town and a parish on the Mississippi River. Some burnt persimmon tree in Acadia Parish is still commemorated by the name of Bayou Plaquemine Brulée.

ACADIAN GIRL with mortar and pestle used for hulling rice. This picture was published in the Crowley *Signal* of January 30, 1904.

19

Le Moulin à Gru:

The Grist Mill

A crude grist mill supplanted the mortar and pestle. The entire mechanism for turning this mill was homemade, and therein lay its more interesting side, for the stones themselves were brought in from elsewhere. Crude as it was, the mill served its purpose. For power, a huge wooden wheel about thirty feet in diameter was set horizontally about six feet above the ground so that its tree-trunk axis or spindle rested and turned in a wooden bearing. In the spindle about three feet from the ground was inserted a pole or beam. When horses were properly hitched to that tongue, they could turn the big wheel as they walked round and round under it. A bull-hide belt then transmitted the power to the nearby pulley, so that for each revolution of the great wheel the mill made about 100 revolutions. Thus the mill was operated by slow-moving horses or oxen to the creaking and groaning of the entire mechanism. That was the *moulin à gru*.

ACADIAN *moulin à gru,* or grist mill, run by horses. This rare photograph
was copied from a special edition of the Crowley *Signal,* May, 1898. It
may be the only photograph of a type of mill which has long since
passed out of existence in the Cajun country.

Not every man could have such a mill. Usually the miller was
an Acadian with a large family. He ground corn for his neighbors for miles around. They usually brought their corn in sacks
by various means—on horseback, in buggies, or on sleds. Occasionally a nearby neighbor carried a small sack of corn on his shoulder.

Saturday was mill day as well as a day for gossip while waiting
for the corn to be ground. Corn was ground for a toll, usually a
fifth measured out before grinding, as the miller did not grind
his own corn at that time. Some millers measured with a parti-
tioned trough; others used a bucket. Little boys sometimes were
sent to the mill, but at some mills it was advisable for a man to
go himself just to keep an eye on the miller while he did the
measuring. Sometimes a greedy miller would "take *all* your corn
and chase you for the sack."

Later, the gasoline engine replaced the oxen and horses. Better
mills that could grind faster were introduced, although some customers said the fast turning mills "burnt up the meal." Nowadays, most of the cornmeal consumed in the Cajun country comes

from grocery stores, but during the thirties a different source of power was used. The mill was mounted on an old automobile chassis, and the motor turned the mill by means of a pulley right on the drive shaft of the car. Quite a menial task for an old Buick motor, but a milestone of progress in getting meal for one's *couche-couche*.

20

Sirop de Batterie,

Acadian Brand

Oᴘᴇɴ kettle sugar cane syrup was eaten in great quantities by all the old Acadians. Few families ate less than a barrel a year, and a family of eighteen children once set a record by eating two hundred gallons of cane syrup in one year. There was plenty of work for the country-style *sucrerie*. Most of the little mills in Acadia Parish were located near some bayou and right at the edge of the woods. Several of them operated for many years on Bayou Plaquemine Brulée, for there was good land for cane, and it was handy to get wood which was always the fuel used for boiling out the cane juice. Any mill out on the open prairie, of which there were only a few, was always at a disadvantage because those millers had to haul their wood in wagons for miles over poor country roads.

The Acadian country millers never went in for making sugar. They made syrup right from the cane juice without taking any

ACADIAN FARMER AND SYRUP MAKER stands by his mill. It is the off season and much of the mill has been dismantled. The cane is crushed between the rollers which are turned by horse power. Note last year's pile of bagasse in the background.

sugar from it. It made a syrup with a strong flavor, but that was the way they liked it. They thought that *sirop de batterie,* put up in jugs, demijohns, and barrels, was better than any thin syrup bought in cans. A miller could convert your patch of cane into syrup on halves. You raised the sugar cane, cut it, and hauled it to the mill, furnished the containers for it, and he did the rest, even to supplying the wood used for fuel, which was very considerable.

The mill itself was quite primitive. The spindles, or rollers, for crushing the cane and extracting the juice were turned by horses, just as Père Labat showed the operation in a drawing he made in the West Indies in 1724. Two hundred years later the Acadians were using the very same system for crushing cane and boiling the juice in open kettles. At some time in the thirties mechanical power replaced the last of the horse mills and, finally, country syrup making passed out completely.

21

Café Noir

ACADIANS parch or roast their coffee and grind it themselves. On a still morning as you drive along a country road in Acadian areas you get the aroma of coffee being parched, and before you lose the aroma from one house you pick up that of the next. You can travel for miles without ever getting away from the aroma of coffee. They say that on Bayou Lafourche you can "smell coffee for forty miles."

Acadians like the *petit noir* (small black), usually called a demitasse, but some want it served in a big cup. They usually don't drink much at a time, but they drink it strong, and they drink it often. No matter where you go in Acadian country, they will be drinking coffee or about to make coffee. Western cowboys talked themselves up a reputation for drinking strong coffee, but Acadians really do. Everybody knows that coffee can keep an

Acadian awake only on one condition; that is, "when he knows there is some and he can't get at it."

"How do you like your coffee," asks Emile, "so it will taste good or so it will hold you up? Some like it strong enough to work on the road. Me, I like it strong enough to 'trow the spoon out of the cup."

Granpère began the day by having his first cup served to him in bed. Then he had coffee before breakfast, at breakfast, and again after breakfast. When he was a young fellow he had ten o'clock coffee, but as he got older he had to have it earlier and earlier. He got up to where he had his ten o'clock coffee at seven-thirty. He said, "I don't want coffee very often—just often enough so that the taste from one cup stays in my mouth until I get the next cup." No wonder coffee rationers were given a rough time by the Acadians! The social workers in the thirties likewise had it rough when they tried to cut down on the family coffee allowance.

> *Le café noir dans un paquet bleu,*
> *Le plus je bois, le plus je veu.*

Black coffee in a blue package,
The more I drink, the more I want.

22

Madame Belizaire
and her Basse-Cour

THE Acadian housewife had some very definite rights in matters pertaining to work, spending money, and such things as raising chickens, and Madame Belizaire was one to take full advantage of hers. The second line of this parody on the Casey Jones song goes far in telling which money was Madame Belizaire's to have and to spend:

> *L'argent à Casey Jones, c'est l'argent de coton,*
> *L'argent à Madame Casey Jones, c'est l'argent des poules,*
> *L'argent à le garçon à Casey Jones, c'est les ouaouaron . . .*

> Casey Jones's money is the cotton money,
> Madame Casey Jones's money is the chicken money,
> Casey Jones's son's money is the bullfrog money . . .

In keeping with the times, Madame Belizaire owned the *basse-cour*, or flock; she attended the chickens; and it was she who spent the money that the chickens and eggs brought in.

Although chicken raising was an old industry on the prairies, Madame Belizaire and her neighbors broke every rule of modern scientific chicken raising. In the spring of the year, when the hens began to lay, a few of them established nests in the small chicken house provided for them; others made nests under the corncrib; and still others took to the weeds and made nests where they laid their eggs and hatched out their chicks. Some of the nests Madame Belizaire found, and others she did not—that is, not until the hens appeared with their little chickens. If the chickens ran to one color, Madame Belizaire thought something should be done about it. To remedy this she traded eggs with the neighbors and thus insured getting a great variety of colors in her flock.

With the hatchings came not only the many-colored chicks, but also hosts of chicken mites. She was always glad to see the chicks, but she hated mites: "I like fleas better than chicken mites." As brooders and incubators were unknown in the old days, the chicks swarmed over the yard, darting here and there under the watchful eyes of the mother hens, and under the care of Madame Belizaire. At night she cooped them up against the night air, rats, cats, and other possible dangers. The approach of a thunderstorm always sent Madame Belizaire scurrying after the chicks to get them into the chicken house, or even into her own house, as there was no telling how much rain might come in a matter of a few minutes.

For feed Madame Belizaire had her boys crack corn with a hand mill, and this sufficed unless she could buy some rice grits for them. Soon the chicks were big enough to eat shelled corn. This she fed to them by merely throwing it out the back door. In no time at all they learned to hang around her back door, and soon some of them found their way into the house. These made nice tame pets.

As would be expected, Creole eggs were fertile, and they were of many colors or, rather, shades. Sometimes Madame took them to the grocery store in her big gourd basket, but at other times she sent one of the boys on horseback with a few dozen eggs tied up in an old flour sack. Still, she had the unrestricted right to say how the egg money would be spent. 'Ti Mile had to account for every cent the eggs brought. One day 'Ti Mile had bad luck. His horse shied and threw him. If you think Madame Belizaire had scrambled eggs for supper you are mistaken. Poor 'Ti Mile broke his arm, but not one egg was even cracked!

Of course, Madame Belizaire sold some of the chickens she raised, that is, depending upon her luck. But there was always a strong demand for her chickens right at home. Sunday dinners called for chicken, and many times she felt obliged to use some of her own chickens for chicken gumbo, which she served on holidays and special occasions. Each of those celebrations took several chickens from her *basse-cour*.

Today the chicken, egg, and broiler business is very different in the Cajun country. Production is streamlined and competition is keen. The young agriculturalists belong to 4-H and FFA clubs, and they learn almost as much about chicken raising as anyone in the business. But Madame Belizaire, her *basse-cour,* and her *l'argent des poules* did not abandon the prairie scene for many years.

23

Fighting Chickens:
Les Coqs Ga-ime

Bᴀᴄᴋ in the thirties, if you had driven along almost any dirt road in the Bosco or Marais Bullard country on a Sunday afternoon, sooner or later you would have seen a gathering of men and boys under some grove of chinaberry trees. The attraction would have been a chicken fight—that is, unless it was a horse race. Both sports were very common in that country from time immemorial, and they still are.

Although every flock of Cajun chickens had some fighting blood in it, it was the chicken specialist who kept the sport going, just as the Mexicans in the Southwest and the Filipinos in California have kept it going. Today a new group has entered into the sport with chickens and cash to back them up. They are the "Texas oil men" who drive over to Cajun country for the sport.

Most fighting roosters seem to be red and black in color, with hooked beaks and long, sharp spurs. They are raised along with other chickens of the country flocks, but when they are big enough to show fight, and start scrapping among themselves and the rest of the chickens, they are caged and kept separate. Put through rigorous training, they are carefully prepared for their careers. Although their own spurs are sharp enough to kill other chickens, man, in his inhumanity to chickens, gives his cocks artificial spurs called gaffs. Whereas a fight under natural conditions drags on, with the gaffs the winner is soon determined.

Formerly the arenas were in the open or under the chinaberry trees, but nowadays some of the more progressive promoters have built shelters that are rather elaborate—at least for the Cajun country. There the high-strung participants battle for life and the animated audience stands or sits and perspires, as the windows are seldom big enough to let in much air.

To the outsider it is the people, not the chickens, who are of greatest interest. To be admitted in the more modern arena or ring, one has to be accepted. And no cameras please—for obvious reasons. Excitement runs high. Betting is carried on in all denominations and with all manner of arrangements. As many tricks as possible are used to accomplish the main purpose—winning. When the fights are over, winning roosters are returned to their cages and taken home. They have lived to fight another day.

24

Acadian Animal Caste

MAN imposes caste systems upon his own species, systems which vary widely with the different races, nationalities, and religions. We all know something about those systems, but we know little of the caste systems which man imposes upon his domestic animals. As we shall see, such systems may be very complex. They may vary, not only with the different species of farm animals, but with different individuals in the same species, and a single animal may pass from one category to another as it lives through several stages of its life in the possession of a single owner.

Among the Acadians the animal caste system was very pronounced. Our hypothetical *petit habitant,* Emile Belizaire, in the year 1915 was a cotton farmer with about forty acres of land. He was using mules to work his land, as were all of his neighbors at that time, and he was following a type of economy that was partly subsistence and partly commercial, with cotton as his main cash crop. He tried to "live at home." He did not have a car, but he had a buggy and wagon. For going to town or visiting, he used a horse hitched to the buggy. For hauling, he used mules hitched to the wagon.

Since Emile is a composite personality, it may be assumed that he owned, among his many animals, all of the ones that are representative of that whole section of the country. In this sketch no attempt is made to show that Acadians treated their animals better or worse than other people treated their animals at that time. Much of this caste system has passed out of existence. The status of the animals has shifted, and the treatment accorded them has changed greatly. Education has been a powerful influence in bringing about the change.

Horses and mules. Three horses in Emile's small herd received priority treatment over all others. They were the stallion, the racehorse, and 'Ti Mile's riding or courting horse. Through good times and bad, these three horses were fed corn and hay in the winter. In the summer they were fed corn and grass, or perhaps corn tops which were brought in by hand to feed them when the grass was short. When all home-produced feed played out, a commercial feed was bought for them. In addition to the special feed, they had the best of it when it came to shelter during rains and cold weather. In summer they were allowed to stand in the shade of the chinaberry trees during the heat of the day. They were kept there, not only for protection against the sun, but so that those who passed in the road could see them, for these three horses were kept intentionally before the public.

After all, the stallion's value depended upon the colts he produced; the racehorse's value depended upon the races he won; and the courting horse had value to 'Ti Mile according to the prestige that he brought his rider. Appearances counted for a great deal, and the horses were expected to come through. "If that horse loses his race Sunday, he goes to the plow on Monday."

Next in order came the buggy horse. He was an older horse, one that was thoroughly dependable and easily managed. He was taken for granted and was the buggy horse for years. He was fed and taken care of, but he never got the special attention accorded the three previously mentioned horses. He held a more stable position in the hearts of the members of the family than did any of the others because of his longer service and the attachment the children had for him. This horse may formerly have been a stallion, a racehorse, or a courting horse, but now he was older and had lost some of his former spirit. He was the horse by which the neighbors recognized Emile's buggy anywhere in the whole neighborhood. This horse was never put up for sale. He was "the old lady's horse."

A step below the buggy horse were the work horses, but they still were ahead of the mules. In winter they were fed only enough to make them serviceable as work horses for the winter and spring plowing. Brood mares fell in a class somewhere near the work horses except in case of a brood mare of racing or some other special stock.

The mules occupied the very lowest place on the equine ladder. They did the most work, and they got the poorest treatment. They were tougher than horses, both in the matter of getting by on little feed and in enduring the hot weather. They made ideal animals for a small farmer who was raising cotton and corn. The crop had to be made, so the poor mules had to keep going, sore shoulders, sore backs, and all. It was like a contest—one in which the mules tried to live through it all to get the crop laid by before the feed played out. It seems that they always made it, and when turned out to pasture, they recuperated rapidly. They went through the same routine year in and year out until old age or disease relieved them of their miseries. In all probability neither they nor the horses ever appreciated the saying: "A fifty-cent whip is worth more than a dollar barrel of corn."

Cattle. The raising of cattle came out of the old vacherie industry, in which half-wild cattle grazed in the open prairie and drank from the coulees and ponds. In the old days they required no care, and with the change in times, it was difficult for many Acadian farmers to realize the actual needs of cattle when confined to small pastures with limited grazing and water resources. There was no cultural heritage which told them that cows must have plenty of clean water and a year-round supply of grass or feed. For a long time Emile's cows had to put up with scorched grass in summer, meager grass in winter, winter cold, summer heat, besides the hosts of flies and mosquitoes. Once when Emile saw milk cows being fed, his remark was, "I know lots of people that would like to get feed like that." Even in the thirties he was keeping altogether too may scrubs, but now, how times have changed!

Hogs. The razorback hog, when penned up and fed little, is not a beautiful hog. Such were Emile's hogs in the summertime. He kept a couple of brood sows which gave him little pigs that were destined to this hard life all summer long. Had they been allowed to roam, they would have ruined all of the crops about. No matter what the size of Emile's pig pen, there was never enough, or any, grass in it. No provision was made for improved pasture for the hogs. Dish water, slop, a little corn, and perhaps some weeds gathered from a turn row kept the hogs alive until fall.

After All Saints' Day, when all crops were supposed to have been gathered, everyone turned his hogs loose. Usually a man's hogs went to his own cornfield, where some corn could be found, and then to the potato patch, where they could root for any potatoes that had not been gathered. The hogs never seemed to stray too far. When they approached a neighbor's house the boys called out the dogs and set them upon the hogs to chase them home. But, all in all, the fall and winter were the best times for the hogs.

The hog fattened for the year's supply of lard presented an interesting case. He was put in a little fattening pen and stuffed with corn for about two months, during which time he converted the feed into a couple of great kettles of lard for Emile. This hog's pen or cage was an elevated and exposed thing. Had he had more room to exercise his lot would not have been so bad, but he suffered from the cold possibly as much as he had suffered from the heat of the sun during the previous summer.

Chickens. Emile was not responsible for the chickens. They were Madame Emile's own property, she took care of them, and it was she who spent the chicken and egg money.

'Ti Mile kept the *coq ga-ime* as his own. He always had a few fighting chickens about the place, either loose or in coops. On Sunday afternoons 'Ti Mile used to go down the road to try out his rooster against some other one of the neighborhood. Sometimes he brought a rooster back, and sometimes he didn't. A rooster had only one chance at it. He had to kill or be killed. No one wanted a loser.

Dogs. Emile's dogs were a mean, nondescript set. They were watchdogs, they would chase any neighbor's hogs off the place, and they helped the boys in hunting rabbits. But Emile used his dogs to chase his own stock as well. He would set the dogs upon his own milk cows if they turned the wrong way, and the more vicious the dogs, the more praise they would draw from their owner. In any combat or conflict which *he* inspired between his dog and any other animal, it was the dog that was cheered. For treeing a cat, even Emile's own cat, he was awarded special commendation. Yet, about the house when the dog was idle, he received little or no care at all. He might even be kicked about. A wandering dog was shot on sight and sometimes Emile would take a shot at a neighbor's dog.

Cats. Cats stood lowest in rank of all of Emile's animals. There never was any intimacy between the children and the cats, nor did they ever get much care. They hunted for themselves and raised their litters. When little kittens became too numerous they were taken out in a sack and dumped on the road. It brought bad luck to kill cats. "Losing" them brought the same results and, besides, it was so much safer.

Even though this economy came out of the old pastoral economy, there was seldom the attachment to animals that the westerner showed for his horse, upon which his life depended. The excellent care given to certain animals was largely a matter of show. "When the horse was fat he was pretty, and when he was poor he was ugly." And when he was ugly he seemed to lose his friends. Even a poor and useless horse was never killed or put out of his misery. One just never killed a horse. And of course, New World French people never ate horse flesh as did their relations in France and Belgium.

STARTING GATE at a two-lane short horse Cajun race track. The tiny jockey who is up on the horse making the practice start is scarcely visible.

25

Cajun Horse Racing

THE matched short horse race is the race of the Acadians of southwest Louisiana. Nowhere else in the United States, or possibly in the world, are the races shorter, the jockeys younger and lighter, or the horses faster. There may be differences in opinion regarding relative velocities of various pieces of horseflesh, but before wagering heavily against the Cajun horses under Cajun racing conditions, one should consult an authority on horses and horse racing. Robert M. Denhardt, in his book *The Horse of the Americas,* which has an important section on the American quarter horse, states that

Louisiana has provided the short track with the fastest horses for the last fifteen or twenty years. Prior to this time Louisiana people came to Texas for their horses. Because of excellent selection and a fortunate choice of stallions, they soon had some really fast Quarter Horses. The modern Louisiana short horse dates back to the entry into Louisiana of a stallion called Dedier, commonly referred to as "Old D. J."

Not too much is known of D. J. It is commonly believed that he was by Henry Star, a Thoroughbred. He was brought into Louisiana by a very shrewd race-horse man, who first brought a stallion into Louisiana by the name of Dewey. Dewey beat the Louisiana champion, a mare known as Louisiana Girl, running 256 yards. The local people then bought Dewey. Two years later the same race-horse man was back a second time with a faster horse, Dedier. He beat Dewey and again sold his horse, Dedier, to Louisiana people. His sons were good, but his glory came through the excellence of his daughters as brood mares. D. J. mares were responsible for Queenie, Effie, Punkin, Black Beauty, Lady Lee, Mae West, Billy Two, Joe Reed, Joe Moore, Babe Ruth, Danger Boy, Poor Boy, and many others. Other stallions besides Dedier helped Louisiana short horses, the greatest of all being Flying Bob, who was raised in Louisiana, living there until the last three or four years of his life. He died in February, 1946, at Richmond, Texas. Other outstanding Louisiana stallions are Duson Horse, Young D. J., Marco Way, and Forester.[1]

The above-named Lady Lee was a notable example of the champions of the Cajun short races. She was bred by the Delahoussaye family of Abbeville and originally was named Louisiana Lady. Her name was later changed to Lady Lee. She ran herself out of competition in Louisiana and was sold to the McKinsey stable in California. Under the new ownership she raced at the best short horse tracks from Texas to California, winning many championships and seldom losing a race. She ran 300 yards in 17.4 seconds to set a world's record and she came back the next day to run the quarter in 22.5 seconds. She was everything that her Abbeville backers had claimed, but she was only one of many fast horses to come out of the Cajun country.[2]

Not only are the horses interesting, but so are the tracks, the jockeys, and the people who frequent the tracks. Distances are not set in yards, furlongs, or miles, but rather in arpents, an arpent being about 193 feet. A common race is four arpents, or 256

[1]Robert M. Denhardt, *The Horse of the Americas* (Norman, 1947), 266-67.
[2]See Nelson C. Nye, "The Lady From Louisiana," *Horse Lover Magazine* (April-May, 1948), 18-19, 44.

yards. A long-distance race, to the Cajuns, is the quarter, or seven arpents.

Since most races are matched races, the tracks usually have only two running lanes. Each lane is paralleled by a board fence to prevent horses from fouling each other or leaving the track. The jockey really has little to do except stick to the horse and urge him on by whipping and yelling. Jockeys ride at catch-weights, so they are seldom weighed. A somewhat bigger and stronger boy warms the horse up before the race, but for the actual race one sees only the youngest and lightest possible jockeys on the horses. Some of them begin riding at the age of six and are all through riding when they reach the age of nine or ten. Some riders are veterans in the second year of riding before their permanent front teeth grow out.

From the bush tracks have come many jockeys who later made good on the big circuits. Of them, Eric Guerin of Maringouin is perhaps best known. Euclid and Ray LeBlanc also came from there. Other Cajun jockeys who broke in to racing as youngsters are the Dubois boys from Kaplan, Dudley Richards of Rayne, R. Strauss of Church Point, Dales Guidry of Lafayette, Charles Billeaud of Erath, L. Castille of Carencro, and Joe Hungerford of Gueydan. Also from Gueydan came Sidney LeJeune. Johnny Delahoussaye of New Iberia and Ray Broussard of Abbeville are also riders from the Cajun country.

To the outsider, probably the most interesting thing about Cajun racing is to be found in the emotions and personalities of the owners, trainers, and those who attend the races. To say that the personnel around the real bush tracks is bilingual is almost an exaggeration, as English is little spoken. Both the Cajuns and the Negroes speak the Cajun dialect, but they lace it with many English words.

It is expected that anything might be done to win a race, and, of course, one should find no fault with any of the tricks except the use of the syringe or needle. This is said to be quite common on tracks where no saliva tests are made. The various injections are said to have magical effects, but one veterinary said that the only effect Cajun horse-hopping has is "to make a man bet more on his horse."

Most of the above should not be condemned; it is common knowledge to all Cajun horsemen. However, the Cajun horseman knows a few other tricks of a more questionable nature. He can tell you how to get a horse into the winner's circle at the city track. First, the dam should be bred so as to foal in the month of October. He will then tell you to register the colt as having been born in January or February. Since the birthday of all race horses is January 1; the advantage is obvious. Colts legitimately registered are, of necessity, two or three months younger than the Cajun colt. To derive further advantage, the mare is bred to a quarter horse stallion rather than a thoroughbred stallion, but the colt is registered as a thoroughbred. The advantage is two-fold in that quarter horses mature earlier and are faster at the shorter distances than the thoroughbreds. It would be too glaring, and therefore too easily detected, if the colt were reared by a quarter horse mare. The colt is first run on the bush tracks. When racing season rolls around in the city, there is the country colt ready to meet the legitimate competition of people whose main purpose is to "improve the breed." After the two-year-old colt finishes the season with a few wins, back to the country he goes, where he may either continue to race or pass into oblivion.

The Cajun country has at times been tremendously interested in harness racing. Both trotters and pacers had their fling, and during the old horse-and-buggy days many a farmer had a fine buggy animal in which he took great pride. These races called for an oval track. Some competition of real quality developed, but, of course, not all racing was confined to the tracks. Many a driver on a country road was challenged by someone else, who naturally took every possible advantage over his rival and did his best to outdistance him.

26

Frog King

How do you get to be
"Frog King?" The late Felix Perres, fire chief of Rayne, became
Frog King of all southwest Louisiana without ever catching a
frog, and yet he richly deserved the honor. He cooked froglegs;
he ate froglegs; he answered questions about froglegs; and he
worked for years to make his brother firemen "frog minded." He
publicized his home town of Rayne as the Frog Market of the
World, which indeed it has been for a long time. At a convention
of firemen in Lafayette, 1,000 of them sat down to a banquet of
one of King Felix's rare treats. To a man, they pronounced it the
most sumptuous feast ever to tempt their palates.

Slowly the world is becoming aware of the fine qualities of
the legs of the Louisiana Jumbo Bullfrog (*Rana catesbiana*), and
restaurants from Rayne to Alaska include on their menus "De-
licious Louisiana Froglegs."

But how did all of this come about? First, the bayous, coulees, ponds, and swamps of south Louisiana make an ideal habitat for the bullfrog. It is there that he develops through the different stages: egg, tadpole, little frog, and finally, big frog. The big frogs have a special way of making themselves known. All who are acquainted with the marsh and bayou country have heard the old bullfrogs vocalizing repeatedly in the deepest of basso-profundo voices:

> Jug o' rum,
> Jug o' rum,
> Bring it here,
> I'll give you some . . . .

Long ago, Acadian boys and young men began catching frogs. While they adapted themselves to many kinds of work, they took especially well to the catching of frogs, and many of them depended upon this form of hunting for their spending money. The very conditions that make life pleasant for the frogs make the catching of them hard and dangerous work. The frogs sit on the banks of bayous and ponds on warm balmy nights. It is then that the hunter has to do his work. Carrying his lantern, he walks in the water a few feet from the bank, for there the bullfrog sits, facing the water. The hunter, with his light, must appear in front of the frog, for if the frog is not blinded by the light—one leap and he is away in the water. But blinded as he naturally is by the light, he is easily picked up and put in the sack. Trudging through the water, which is infested with snakes, turtles, and almost anything that lives in and about wet places, the hunter follows a dangerous existence. In the old days, all of them went barefoot. Mosquitoes, gnats, thorns, briars, and even barbed wire, tended at times to make life miserable for him, but frogs brought money.

The frog business, like so many others, is always being modernized. Packing plants with the most modern of cold storage systems, attractive packing, and advertising all play a part in today's frog business. As the demand for frogs has increased, the supply has decreased. Naturally, frog-farming will be the answer and, no doubt, in time frog farms will make possible the marketing of frogs in unlimited quantities. Biology classes and their laboratories provide great and continuous demand for these denizens of the bayous and still give some of the Cajun boys a chance to make a little money. Whether frogs are wanted for the laboratory, the table, or the jumping ring, the Louisiana Jumbo Bullfrog is still the favorite. If Felix Perres were living today, he would undoubtedly smack his lips and say, *"Ah, les ouaouaron— c'est le merveilleux, hein?"*

SIDNEY ARCENEAUX (second from left) and his *boucherie de campagne*. This view was taken on a Friday afternoon during the spring of 1935. By daylight the next morning the goggle-eyed steer had been slaughtered, dressed, and cut up into portions of meat for all the members of the co-operative. Although the butchery was located at the roadside, few visitors to the Acadian country ever saw the plant in operation. "We always kill early and give them their meat so they can go home and go to work."

27

Cajun Co-operatives

L_A boucherie de cam-_
pagne, the country butchery, was the main co-operative of the
prairie Acadians, who were a gregarious people noted for co-
operation and affability. The butchery fitted perfectly into their
way of life, for it gave them a steady and dependable supply of
meat all through the hot summer weather, back when there was
no country refrigeration. Furthermore, it operated when their
cattle were fattest and hogs poorest. All during the winter they
could eat pork, for it was then that the hogs were fattest.

Although these butcheries had operated in the Cajun country
from time out of mind, few townspeople or travelers through
that country ever knew much about them. The reason for their
sketchy knowledge was that the butcher had done his work, dis-
tributed the meat to twenty-four, or in some cases, forty-eight,
participants, and they had all gone home by five or six o'clock in

the morning. After that hour there was little to see except the shed for his table, chopping block, and scales; a little pen where the animal spent his last night; and a raised crossbar on which the beef was hoisted for dressing. There really was not very much for a traveler to see, even though it was all adjacent to the road or easily accessible from the road.

As soon as the spring grass had made the cattle fat enough for slaughter, the butcher called his regular and prospective customers together to draw dates for their turns at furnishing the beef. The man drawing number one led off by "pushing his beef to the pen" on the following Friday, and the co-operative was under way. The other twenty-three participants followed in the order of the numbers they had drawn from the hat, so that each had his turn at "pushing the beef" and each got his ten pounds of meat on the twenty-three consecutive Saturdays. The butcher, for his work, received fifteen pounds of meat and a soup bone. Of course, he furnished no beef.

The butcher had his responsibilities. First, he had to inspect the beef, because "we didn't want no sack of bones to go through." Secondly, he and his sons had to get up at midnight to do the slaughtering, skinning, and dressing. Thirdly, the butcher cut up the meat and divided it into twenty-three little piles in such a manner as he considered fair to all of the customers, who had been his friends and customers for many years. He had to remember to give each some meat from the better cuts and some from the poorer cuts and to apportion out the soup bones fairly. He was equal to the task, and by dawn, which was about 4:00 A.M., he was ready.

The neighbors came in buggies, on horseback, in wagons, on foot, and even in automobiles. Various reasons have been given for the early arrival. One is that they wanted to get home to get in a full day's work. Another was that they wanted to get home with the meat before the weather warmed up. But possibly the real reasons were that they wanted to get *good* meat, and they wanted to come early and stay until it was over, in order to pick up the neighborhood news and gossip.

For years the town meat markets fought to outlaw the country butcheries, but with little success. To be sure, the co-operatives were not screened, nor were there concrete floors in the little sheds as the law requires, but the butchers pointed out that they did not have to be screened, as everything was all finished before daylight, and there were no flies about during the night. "If you padlock my shed, I'll kill out on the open prairie." And that was that. What can a man-made law do against such persistence when the folkway has been handed down from generation to generation and has worked for the economic and social satisfaction of so many people for such a long time? The *boucherie de campagne* probably came in when cattlemen began to pay attention to whose steer was slaughtered on the prairies, and it passed out when better transportation and modern refrigeration came in. The home freezer did something the law could not do.

The *piocherie,* or hoeing bee, was more of a social co-operative than the *boucherie de campagne.* The latter was systemized, and it was run on a definite plan. The hoeing bee was held merely for the unfortunate fellow who fell sick or had some other misfortune which kept him from hoeing his crop. Normally it was due to a condition over which he had no control.

For a deserving person whose cotton was being taken by grass, a *piocherie* was organized by the neighbors. They initiated the move, sent out the word and invitation to the others, and on the appointed day they turned up with their hoes. By pitching in and working for a day, they could hoe the entire crop and save it from the grass and weeds.

For all of this the owner of the crop made no cash payment. He tried to be a gracious host and do right by his good neighbors. He and his wife saw to it that the workers had a good dinner— dinner being the noon meal. Gumbo, roast goose, roast pig, or chicken usually made the main part of such a meal. For a man of extremely poor circumstances the neighbors sometimes furnished the dinner or would "carry their buckets." In cases where the host had been laid up with typhoid fever, the neighbors either carried their buckets or dashed home for dinner. Whether an obligation was incurred when one was benefited by a hoeing bee depended upon circumstances. The farmer might return the favors of his neighbors in kind when they suffered a misfortune.

Should you begin shingling your house during a particularly slack season when the neighbors were idle, as likely as not several of them would come over with their tools for a *couvrage,* or shingling bee. The activity broke the monotony of loafing at home, and the workers enjoyed the refreshments which invariably were served on such occasions.

Helping a neighbor in time of need was giving a *coup de main,* or lending a hand. This was quite different from giving a *coup de poing,* which is a "lick with the fist!"

The story is told that at one *couvrage,* a fellow boasted that he had learned to shingle from his old man by *"des coups de tap sur la joul"*—that is, by taps on the jaw. The comeback to that was, *"Il ne t'a pas tapé assez"* (he didn't slap you enough).

The *écosserie,* or hulling bee, was most common in the days when cotton grew tall and rank and shaded the bolls, so that the hulls rotted without opening the cotton clear, white, and fluffy. When circumstances made picking too slow, and more rain was in view, it was a common custom to "break bolls," that is, pick hulls and all and take the cotton to the house. Then while it was raining, or at night, the whole family could sit around and separate the cotton from the broken hulls.

It was just such a condition as this that called for a hulling bee. Of course, this was the ideal setting for conversation. Food and coffee were served, and if they finished early enough, sometimes there was time for dancing. For being benefited by an *écosserie* the host obligated himself only to the extent that he should take part when the neighbors gave theirs.

Nowadays the cotton is better. It matures earlier and loses much of its foliage, so there is little benefit derived from hulling. Other excuses for getting together have to be thought up, and they usually are.

The *banco* is thought to be of Spanish origin. It is a gathering for a game of chance either for the benefit of an organization, or a person, or just because some enterprising fellow worked up one. At a church *banco,* individuals used to contribute commodities such as chickens, ducks, geese, and fruit, and they played for these prizes. If the church wanted a new sidewalk or some repairs or improvements, that would easily be sufficient cause for holding a *banco*.

A sick neighbor sometimes bought a barrel of apples or oranges and sold them at a high rate to his neighbors, who then gambled for them. As they lost to each other they bought more; often he sold the entire lot in one evening at a profit. The oranges usually were brought from the *chenières* where they had been grown, so the orange *banco* was at least one method of importing oranges.

Seldom would a man who attended a *banco* want to return home and face his family empty-handed. If he lost, he would simply buy more fruit to take home, and thus save face with his wife and children.

When all of the roads were dirt roads and there was no efficient national, state, or parish plan for working the roads, each farmer was required to contribute two or three days work per year with a team. The plow required two pairs of horses or mules and the grader or pusher required about six pairs. Each man drove his own team and the whole endeavor became quite a social gathering.

The poorer neighbors and hired men or croppers, who owned no teams, contributed only their own labor. Their job was to shovel out the places that the grader missed in turning around at the end of a section. There was always a leader or boss man, usually an older man or a fat man. All of the little bridges over the ditches had to come out, so the men just lifted them out, but each farmer replaced his own without help.

This way of working the road was followed for decades, but usually it was not very satisfactory because of the work being done at the wrong time of the year, the rough way in which it was done, and the wrong conceptions of how to work a dirt road. With the coming of gravel roads, the work was done on a commercial basis by governmental organizations. No one regretted the passing of the old type of work on the "public road."

A SECTION LINE "public road" in the Cajun country. The catalpa trees shown were planted for shade and for fence posts.

28

Contracts and Bargains

V<small>ERBAL</small> contracts and
bargains were an important part of the old Acadian culture. A
great many of the old mores still applied in the thirties, but after
World War II, with considerable change from mule to tractor
power, with larger operations, higher prices, and the introduction of more sweet potato production, dairying, and other forms
of diversification, there have been great changes. Modernization
has caused many of the old arrangements to decline in use or
even go out completely, but from the historical point of view,
they may still be of interest.

The people of the cotton section, perhaps best typified by the
western part of Lafayette Parish and the eastern part of Acadia
Parish, engaged in many types of contractual agreements, deals,
and bargains which, in the old days, were seldom written down.
This is a section of small farmers and croppers rather than one

of plantation owners, and the people are to a considerable extent subsistence farmers. Cotton has long been the main commercial crop, but still the area has not been one in which large amounts of cash were handled. Instead, they developed a system based largely upon shares and tolls for services rendered, rather than one in which there were cash charges.

The writer recalls many of the arrangements, the following being quite characteristic and still in use at the present time:

Octave: "Could I have that place on thirds?"

Hypolite: "Yes."

Octave: *"Bien."*

The above words spoken by Octave the sharecropper and Hypolite the landlord are all that are necessary for making a contract which in other parts of the country might have required the services of two lawyers with power of attorney and the services and stamp of a notary public. But in the local folkways of the people, this was a bargain. It stands, as have thousands of others made in just as casual a manner.

Cropping on thirds. In the above contract the landlord had a place of thirty or so acres which he had let out previously on shares. The departing occupant, having decided to move on, left the vacancy which Octave was now to occupy. Landlord Hypolite was now to supply the cropland, some land to be used for pasture for Octave's livestock, a house, a barn and structures that passed for a chicken house and other outhouses, and the fences. He was to pay the taxes on the land and, at the end of the year, he was to receive a third of the produce of the place.

Octave's part was more involved. He knew that he was to move into the house and start making his crop. For this he brought to the place all of his possessions. These included a pair of mules, a horse, a wagon and buggy, a couple of cows and a calf, a few pigs, and some chickens. He also brought his tools, such as a plow, harrow, cultivator, and planter, besides seed and feed. The latter he had saved out of his previous year's crop. With these, he and his family began the new year on the new place, making a crop in which he supplied all of the labor and bore all of the expenses.

In the fall of the year he gave Hypolite a third of all of the produce, such as cotton, corn, and sweet potatoes. He gave no part of the increase in hogs or chickens, but through the year Madame Octave took some gunny sacks full of vegetables and melons over to the Hypolite home, for which she was always thanked. This produce was never weighed or counted. In the above type of contract the share cropper has the right to say how he shall work the crop. Only when a cropper works on halves does the landlord have the right to supervise the making of the crop and say how it shall be worked.

In some communities December 1 is the date before which either the landlord or the tenant must express his desire to break off, while in others the date is as early as August 15. If the deadline passes without any expression by either, it means that there will be no change for the next year. The departing cropper is not obligated to move before the first of the new year, but usually he moves as soon as his new place is open.

Cropping on halves. Had Octave taken the place on halves, Hypolite would have been obligated to furnish everything except the labor in making the crop, but in this arrangement, and in this one alone, the landlord retains the right to say how the crop shall be worked. Nor does the cropper receive the right to plant more corn than cotton. Landlords are well acquainted with the fact that their expenses are about the same for an acre of corn as for an acre of cotton, and that less labor is required and the return is less in the planting of corn. A compromise is made in which an equal acreage is planted in corn and cotton—this also makes a satisfactory crop rotation. "Some landlords hardly allow a half-man land enough for garden and sweet potatoes, nor let him plant much corn, and *never* allow enough land to be used for pasture unless it is rice land that he wants cleaned up."

Free use of the landlord's team by the cropper on the road for going to town or going visiting is something against which landlords guard. Yet the cropper uses the landlord's team for hauling firewood from the woods. But for this favor, the cropper must ask for the use of the team each and every time he wants to haul a load.

Working on fourths. In a small number of cases croppers worked on fourths. In this type of agreement, the landlord furnished *only the land*, and for this he received a fourth of the crop. Since the cropper had to furnish his own house, in addition to those things which he furnished while working on thirds, the system made for a greater degree of permanency; in fact, some croppers working "on the fourth" remained on the same places for several decades. The "school lands" were commonly let out on fourths, as were a few large estates in which the land owners usually lived elsewhere. It is obvious that the smaller the landlord's share in the crop, the more remote are his relations with the cropper, and the less he knows about what takes place on his land.

Miscellaneous fees. The Acadian who had his corn ground at a country mill usually paid the miller a toll of one-fifth. Corn was never ground for a cash fee.

Cotton ginners used to gin cotton for the seed. In case they did gin for a cash fee, the sum was taken from the sale price of the cotton. The landlord, not the cropper, usually handled the business of getting cotton ginned and sold. As one farmer stated it: "The ginning service and the seed value are reckoned in money, and a small balance is returned to the owner of the cotton."

In the old days, when the operator of a *sucrerie* made syrup from your sugar cane crop, he charged you a half and he furnished the wood. If you chose to furnish the wood for boiling the juice and cooking the syrup, he reduced his toll to one third.

For making whips out of raw cowhides, a country blacksmith charged half of the whips the hide would make.

For weaving wool into blankets, a weaver charged one half.

For cutting wood, one load for the owner of the woods and one for the man who did the cutting.

For butchering the landlord's hog, the cropper was usually given the head and the "innards," depending upon the likes and dislikes of the landlord and his wife.

For (illegally) treating a sick person, a "voodoo treater" usually received a gift. Although he could not legally collect, fear of reprisal through "voodoo" or "gris-gris" probably made his percentage of collections fairly high. Of course, those treaters also attempted to cure animals of such ailments as anthrax, blind staggers, lockjaw, and warts.

For teaching the catechism to the children of the neighborhood, an elderly lady would usually receive a gift from each at the time they made their first communion.

Rice country arrangements. The rice country was settled mainly by "Americans" from the wheat country of the Middle West, and its economy has little in common with the small-scale farming of the Acadians of the cotton country. Rice raising was on a large scale from the start, and in it the renter or tenant is the person of importance; it is the landlord who drops into the subordinate position.

The operator, in this type of agriculture, may give a fifth of the crop for land, and usually he gives a fifth for water, but otherwise he is on his own. He operates on a cash basis for most arrangements—he pays wages in cash and he pays so much for the hauling of rice or so much per sack for threshing, in case he does not have his own equipment. The general rule is that the rice farmers are big operators who work on a commercialized, or even industrialized, basis.

In keeping with the modern trend, science enters more and more into agriculture. The use of commercial fertilizers and insecticides are musts. The old and the modern, however, continue to exist side by side.

29

Courtship and Marriage

GETTING married at an early age has always been a Cajun custom. In the old days, if a girl wasn't married before she was twenty, she was *une vieille fille,* or old maid. Many of them, by the time they were twenty, had three or four children. Yet at those tender ages, they knew almost as much about keeping house as their mothers did. The grooms, in most cases, were several years older than their brides. They knew how to grow cotton and corn and take care of stock about as well as their fathers did, so why wait? Somehow they managed to get along, didn't they?

Acadian girls, in the old days, were exposed to few of the besetting sins of life. They were, as is the case with many girls of Latin descent, always under the watchful eyes of their mothers. Most frequently, courtships began at dances, for in the home the girls played a rather subordinate role. Let us suppose that a young man called upon a neighbor to inquire about a cow, and the head of the household invited him in for coffee. The mother spoke to the caller, but usually the daughter paid no attention, outwardly, whatsoever. She was "too busy" with the housework. Her work was a means of keeping occupied so as to not feel ill at ease. She may have been barefooted and in her commonest dress. Also, she may have been wearing her *garde-soleil,* or sunbonnet, by which she could keep her face concealed—that is, when she wanted to.

Fresh coffee was soon made and served while the men talked about cattle, or anything that came to mind. But on Saturday night, the fellow made up for lost time. He danced repeatedly with the girl. After the playing of "Home Sweet Home," he walked with her and the family to their wagon or carriage. Next morning he was just at the right place at the right time to walk with the girl from the church door to the carriage, again, of course, along with the family. From here on, coincidences occurred regularly, and everyone knew just what was developing.

Sunday afternoon visits became a regular event. The young couple would sit in the kitchen by the hour, while the rest of the family sat in the adjoining rooms—with the doors open. Engagements were of different lengths, but if a girl was to be married by the time she was seventeen, courtship had to be brief. Any caller without serious matrimonial intentions was not giving a girl a fair deal. Although she may not have said so, the girl wanted the attention of only eligible and likely prospects. Her family concurred in that feeling.

Customarily, the prospective groom asked his fiancée's parents for her hand in marriage. Thursday night was the time for this step. When the young man called on that night all dressed up in his best clothes, everyone knew his precise mission. The little speech was always well rehearsed, but they say many a fellow stammered through it. Even the most incoherent speech of that kind was understood.

Oneziphore Guidry's *fais-dodo,* where many an Acadian dance was held.

The license was secured the next Saturday, and on Sunday the bans were read in church. For three consecutive Sundays the announcement of their intent was read. On the next Saturday the wedding took place.

The week preceding the wedding was one of great excitement. The women of the family worked on the trousseau and wedding dresses. They fixed up the house and prepared food for a great feast. The popularity of the girl, the status of the family, and the number of nearby kinfolks determined, to a great extent, the number of guests and the amount of food to be served. But no matter how much of the father's stock of chickens, ducks, geese, and pigs it took, he was always glad to feed the entire crowd because all of this was a measure of importance and popularity. He was glad to show the hospitality and they were glad to accept his hospitality—even down to his last chicken. Serious illness or death were the only possible "regrets" for not accepting the cordial invitations.

Most weddings were held in the late afternoon at the church in the nearest town. As buggies were the main means of transportation, any wedding of importance called for a long procession of them. As they left the bride's house, the bride and her father rode in the first buggy. The groom and his father rode in the second, and other relatives followed. Mothers usually did not attend those weddings: "They are too sad." On arriving at the church, the horses were hitched to the racks, and the crowd assembled at the front of the church.

The ceremony was followed by the exciting, helter-skelter ride back home. The newlyweds led off in a buggy drawn by the fastest horse available. The two fathers rode in the second buggy, which was also drawn by a fast horse. From there on, it was anybody's race. There was some drinking on the return trip, and always there would be an accordion or two to liven up the procession.

Mountains of food, omnipresent at any Acadian gathering, were always on hand, even at the humblest home.

For a week before the wedding, all of the nearby neighbors had refrained from their regular work in order to have things prepared for the feast. The women, colored and white alike, had gathered at the bride's house for three days, shelling nuts and baking cakes. At least a half-barrel each of sugar and flour were used in baking cakes. On the fourth day the men accompanied their wives. This day was devoted to the dressing of meats. For the wedding of my grandma, Miss Gadric Arceneaux, about seventy-five years ago, thirteen young pigs, fifteen geese, five turkeys, and a two-year-old calf were killed.

On the morning of the wedding day, the cooking had long begun. Men barbecued out of doors while the women busied themselves preparing the roasts, baking and broiling the fowl, giving the finishing touches to the salads, and, last but not least, baking the biscuits. Plump dumplings and spicy rice jambalaya, old Acadian favorites, were also part of the feast. A long table, twenty-five or thirty feet long and about five feet wide, was placed in a shady spot out of doors. It was set over and over until everyone had been served. And there never was a time when there wasn't enough food.[1]

[1]For this description of an old-time wedding feast I am indebted to Edna Mae Arceneaux, who, while a pupil at Rayne High School in 1936, gathered the information for me.

The *bal de noce,* or wedding ball, followed. The wedding crowd augmented the regular Saturday-night crowd at the *fais-dodo* hall. That made it truly a festive occasion.

The bride was not a bride for long. She was soon the mother of several children, and before she was out of her thirties she was several times a grandmother.

They say that there was a custom by which a girl could "sack" an unwanted suitor. She would send the unfortunate man a little coat that would fit into an envelope, either by mail or by an acquaintance, and that meant that he was through. The custom gave rise to a little song:

> Ce n'est pas la bague
> J'ai regretté;
> C'était le capot
> Que ma belle m'a donné.

> It is not the ring
> That I regretted;
> It is the coat
> My sweetheart gave me.

But, judging by the number of marriages among the very young Acadians, not many coats were ever sent.

An interesting adjunct to some Acadian weddings was the "charivari." Any widow, widower, or even old bachelor who got married in the old days in Cajun country inwardly expected to get a charivari—that is, unless he, or she, was a social outcast. The marriage of a widow to a widower called for a big celebration, so when the widower Theophile and the widow Celestine slipped off to New Orleans and got married, they suspected that something extraordinary would be done upon their return to town.

No one knew on what train they would return, but on the other hand, at least a dozen people always turned out to meet the train. It was just one of those things that people did to pass the time of day and to get news. But still the newlyweds thought they could get off the train and slip over to Theophile's house, and the celebration could come later. The neighbors could "surprise" them at night.

By coincidence, the newlyweds returned on the very same train that brought from New Orleans the new school teacher who was several days late in reporting. During the first few days of school the other teacher of the two-teacher school thought it fitting to welcome her new co-worker with a parade so there were all of the children lined up in two rows with the smallest ready to lead them and the taller ones in the rear. They all carried flags, and the welcome was a hearty one.

The modest young teacher, somewhat abashed at seeing the entire group of children, permitted most of the attention to be fixed upon the newlyweds. Theophile had not expected anything like this. Never before had anyone ever been greeted by all of the school children in this manner. He rose to the occasion and thanked them and went down the line shaking hands with every one of them. The teachers and all of the other adults began to move in the direction of the main street. In unorganized fashion the adults walked along, followed by the children in their two straight lines. At the post office, the street forked. Toward the right was the school house; toward the left was Theophile's house. The teachers took the right-hand road, and the children, led by the smallest, took the left-hand road. It was not until the entire student body had gotten strung out on the wrong road that the teachers realized that in another moment all would be lost. The older teacher ran over to the head of the parade, unceremoniously seized the little fellow by the hand and got the parade headed back toward the school house. For the new teacher, not all of the days were as exciting as her first. For the newlyweds, a big charivari was held that night. The entire neighborhood turned out and beat tin tubs in front of the house until they were invited in for one of the biggest feasts the town had ever seen.

30

Fais-Dodo

Dancing has always been the favorite amusement of the Acadians. Throughout most of their stay in Louisiana, they have held private dances in their homes, but it is the public country dance which they call a *fais-dodo* that is of most interest here. A single fiddler or accordion player may have furnished the music for the private dance, but the *fais-dodo* demanded a band of several pieces. As might be expected, the *fais-dodo* has to a great extent superseded the private dance, and that Saturday night and Sunday night feature is the great attraction of the rural Acadians.

Long ago it was written of the Acadians of Grande Pointe on the east bank of the Têche:

They keep up the old Creole custom of having neighborhood balls every Saturday night. The balls are generally attended by sons and daughters of the small Creole farmers who work all day and dance at night. There are not less than sixty fiddles and fiddlers in this settlement.

They are a merry people; and those who think that the young ladies don't know how to arrange their hair and primp for the ballroom, so as to make themselves look attractive to the beaux, are simply mistaken.

With modifications, what was written a century ago is true today, but the old-timers would rather tell about how things were done in their day. They tell how dances were announced and invitations sent out along the bayous. In the "street village" form of settlement, where all the houses fronted the bayou, whoever was to give a dance merely stood on his front porch and shouted up and down the bayou, telling the neighbors to pass the word along. It was as effective as using a telephone, yet no one had to leave his own house. They say that by actual test, a message was sent for forty miles along Bayou Lafourche without anyone leaving his porch.

On the prairies, settlements were more scattered, but word always got around in time, so that any family with eligible daughters was ready to go when Saturday night came. People went to dances on horseback, in buggies, in wagons, and even on foot. In the old days some of the wealthier families went to dances in a type of carriage called a *calèche*.

The grandparents and the grandchildren alike attended many of the old dances, the former to watch and gossip, the latter to sleep and cry. The old folks always managed to keep busy with the local news and gossip, while the babies soon became occupied in an entirely different way. As soon as they dropped off to sleep, they were put on big beds in a room in the back. There they either slept or cried, usually with less attention than they were accustomed to at home. The term *fais-dodo,* go to sleep, is said to have originated this way.

The young folks occupied the middle of the floor, with the girls getting the strictest supervision and chaperoning from their mothers and the older women. No girl could ever leave a dance

THE RAYNE-BO RAMBLERS standing in front of a *fais-dodo* in Rayne in 1936. They are, from left to right, Eric Arceneaux, Louis Arceneaux, and Leroy (Happy Fats) LeBlanc. The Ramblers made many phonograph recordings, and "Happy Fats" became famous as a singer of ballads of many kinds.

hall, once she had entered, until she left with her parents after the last waltz. "If a girl ever leaves the dance hall without her mother, she can never come back in." That was the unwritten law, more strictly enforced than almost any of the written laws. Some of the old folks tell regretfully of the passing of that custom. "Times ain't like they used to be."

Pop was the common refreshment, and it was always sold inside. The boys and men went outside where stronger refreshments, sometimes legitimate and sometimes bootleg, were indulged in. "His whiskey was so bad I had to shut my eyes to drink it."

The conduct of the men sometimes was as free as that of the girls was restricted. Practical jokes were different back in the horse-and-buggy days. You might find that the front and rear wheels of your buggy had been reversed. Partial cutting of stirrup straps and rough trimming of horses' manes and tails led to fights if the culprits were discovered. Otherwise those things were uproariously funny.

The little band of musicians made an essential part of any *fais-dodo,* yet they were not always safe from flying pop bottles. In a few of the rougher sections during the thirties it was customary to set the musicians up in a little elevated cage protected by chicken wire from bottles and other missiles, so that they could play any kind of music they chose to play. It seems that one of the main causes of trouble was the all-important choice of music to be played. Many a fight was started by a dispute over whether a waltz or two-step should be played.

Only the oldest of the Acadians can now remember when anything but the modern dances such as waltzes, one-steps, and two-steps were danced, but some of them will tell you about a dignified square dance called the *Lancier Acadien,* or the Acadian Lancers, which was the opposite number of the Anglo-Saxon square dances.

For the National Folk Festival held at Dallas, Texas, in 1936, Mr. Fred Decuir of New Iberia trained a group of young Acadians in the entire five parts of this dance, which they performed in a most graceful and delicate manner at Dallas as well as at many gatherings in southwest Louisiana. They danced to the music of Mr. Wade Bernard and his band from St. Martinville.

Mr. Bernard's band had purposely kept up the playing of the old dance tunes, and for the National Folk Festival Program in 1936 it played five different moods of music for the five parts which likewise were danced differently, as indicated by their names or titles:

Première Partie . . . . L'Avance
Seconde Partie . . . . Petit Salut
Troisième Partie . . . . Grand Salut
Quatrième Partie . . . . Les Visites
Cinquième Partie . . . . Grande Chaîne

If occasion demanded, Mr. Bernard's band could also oblige with music for the *polka du salon,* a mazurka, an array of waltzes, one-steps, two-steps, and another square dance called

Les Variétés, the latter being danced in four parts to music of four distinctively different types. Still another Acadian dance of a former time was the "jilliling" (a two-step), reportedly named for Jenny Lind.

A wedding dance was the *bal de noce.* That was a special attraction, and it was to the advantage of the operator of the *fais-dodo* to have the *bal de noce* of a popular couple at his hall. Some couples pointed with pride to the fact that they had been paid to have their wedding ball at a certain dance hall. It was a mark of distinction and a measure of popularity. Of course, there was an admission fee. With the great numbers of relatives and friends on both sides of the family, one can easily see the practicality of the investment.

The *fais-dodo* as a building was far less impressive than the *fais-dodo* as an institution. It might be taken for a barn or a warehouse. It had a reasonably good pine floor, wooden benches all the way around, wooden shutters for the windows on all sides, and not much else except a room with a bed or two for babies, a card room for the men who were not dancing, and a refreshment stand. Outside, a distinctive feature, of course, was an abundance of hitching racks where the horses were tied.

Everyone worked through the week in anticipation of the Saturday night dance at the *fais-dodo.* Old Baptiste's daughters camouflaged themselves in the cotton fields in order to appear at their best on the dance floor. Baptiste's daughters were all very pretty, there were six of them, and they were all of cotton-hoeing age. This last qualification Old Baptiste prized above all others, as he was getting old and his boys were still too young to work much in the field. In the spring those girls chopped cotton "from sun to sun," with only a few hours off in the middle of the day when the sun was hottest. From Monday through Friday, except when it rained, you could see the girls going up and down the rows, hoeing Baptiste's cotton.

With them, hoeing cotton and dancing were the main activities, so they planned their clothing accordingly. Of course the result was two entirely different get-ups. Since their arms and hands were bare at the dance, the girls wore long sleeves and gloves while hoeing. And because they wore shoes and stockings to the balls, it was all right for them to go barefooted while hoeing cotton. These rules were fundamental, except for those applying to face and neck. They were not to be sun tanned under any circumstances. That is where the *garde-soleil,* or sunbonnet, came in. The back and sides of each bonnet had a big flap or curtain which draped over the shoulders, shutting out the air and sunshine. Slats sewed in the top of each bonnet caused them all to stick out in front, narrowing their field of vision to a minimum. Likewise, an intruder could walk completely around each of Old Baptiste's daughters while they were hoeing and never get so much as a glimpse of a single face—that is, if they didn't want to see them. The disguise was complete.

But how different Saturday night was from Monday morning! How drab they had looked in the field, and how sweet and fair they looked on the dance floor! Their soiled and tanned feet of the week days may have rebelled at pinching shoes on Saturday night, but if they did, it never showed while they danced. More than one of Baptiste's daughters took off her shoes and stockings as soon as she left the dance hall to go home, whether on foot or in a wagon. The dust or cool mud of the road served as balm to many a tired foot. Thoughts of the ball lingered, but reality could not be avoided. On Monday morning, it was back to the camouflage and the cotton patch.

Acadians still like to dance, but today there is little in their dancing that is different from dancing seen anywhere from Florida to California.

31

Music and Singing

Dancing calls for music, so there has always been a demand for music on the prairies. But among the Acadians there was practically no singing except at dances and for dancing.

Their songs were of the people. They were simple, quite repetitious, and without strong beginnings or endings. They were played before they were ever recorded or written down, and generally the people do not know who composed them. They definitely fall in the folk song class.

The music is ideal for playing with the instruments at hand: the accordion, fiddle, guitar, and the little steel triangle. The most important of these was the accordion. Theirs was music "of the accordion, by the accordion, and for the accordion." By the device of "turning the verses" (a way of playing the tune over between the verses), a song could be made to last long enough for a dance.

In the old bands the accordion player was the leader and main singer, but other musicians took turns at singing. Incidentally, the singers never sing parts or in unison. They sing as soloists only.

In all of Louisiana, it probably is on the prairies that Acadian folk music has survived best. Even at the present time, Acadian music is not merely a relic and museum piece for it is a vital part of the folk culture of the people. The little Acadian bands are in active demand for several nights of playing each week. Each *fais-dodo,* or dance hall, has its schedule of dances, and each engages a different Acadian band for each dance that is scheduled during the week.

Various students of American folkways and music have studied Cajun music, but there can be little doubt that the best informed person on Acadian folk songs is Irène Whitfield Holmes of Lafayette. She was in the fortunate position of having lived in the country between Rayne and Duson and having learned French, music, and some Acadian songs at an early age. Likewise she was fortunate in having had the proper ancestry and connections. From that background and with a great deal of hard work, she wrote a master's thesis at Louisiana State University, and the University Press published it in 1939 under the title *Louisiana French Folksongs.* In this important work are the music, French words, and phonetic pronunciations of one hundred and one songs. Many of them are Louisiana-French, others are in the Creole of the French-speaking Negroes, and forty-eight of them she listed as being Acadian. Of these, eighteen are definitely about love and marriage, and a great many others among them touch on those two important topics. Other Acadian songs tell about people, places, animals, the Civil War, the jug at the pommel of the saddle, and even about going to Texas, the Ultima Thule of long ago.

This writer was chairman of the Louisiana section of the National Folk Festival held in Dallas, Texas, in 1936. Members of the little Acadian band which played there were Lawrence Walker, accordion player; Aldus Broussard, fiddler; Sidney Broussard, fiddler; Junior Broussard, guitar player; Norris Mire, guitar player; and Evelyn Broussard, triangle player and singer. Walker and Aldus Broussard also were singers, and Elmore Sonnier, an educated and trained Cajun singer from Scott, was a special soloist. The little band was so different and proficient in its folk playing that it was popular wherever it played at the festival. No less an authority on folk music than Alan Lomax commented that "Aldus was the best example of folk talent in the whole festival."

With the coming of the phonograph and radio, one would have forecast the doom of Acadian music, but it didn't work that way. Following the initial impact which was quite severe, the musicians followed the motto of the politicians: "If you can't lick 'em, jine 'em."

First to record was now-famous singer and accordion player, Joe Falcon of Rayne. About 1926 he recorded "Allons à Lafayette," or "Let's Go to Lafayette," for an apprehensive recording company. Once the recording hit the market of south Louisiana, Acadians bought several records at a time so they would never be without one, no matter what happened. A new era had opened up. Other singers and recording companies went into the business of recording Acadian folk songs for the south Louisiana market.

With the advent of radio, amplifiers, electric guitars, and other technical changes, at least some bad effects were to be expected. One of these was the influence of the applause meter. After a few years of Major Bowes and his amateur programs, one can only estimate the damage done to performers who had been practicing a purely folk art.

When Acadians began to run out of their own songs, they borrowed others. "Red River Valley," "Lulu's Back in Town," "Casey Jones," and many other well-known songs have been recorded in Cajun French, for they went into the practice of making up new English words for old American songs. Joe Falcon and his wife, the late Cleoma Breaux, recorded nearly a hundred songs in French, and there have been many singers from the prairie area to record the various kinds of songs.

Dr. Harry Oster's article, "Acculturation in Cajun Folk Music," published in *The McNeese Review,* winter issue of 1958, effectively points out how other songs were incorporated into the Acadian pattern and made a part of supposedly Acadian singing. He cites the translation of the song "My Good Ol' Man," which he recorded in 1957 as sung by Mrs. Rodney Frugé and Savy Augustine of Mamou. This writer has a Columbia recording (15301-D) (146908) of the same song which is undated but which was an old copy even in the middle 1930's. It is entitled "Le Vieux Soulard Et Sa Femme," ("The Old Drunkard and His Wife") and vocals are by Joe Falcon and Cleoma Breaux, whom he later married. The Columbia and Oster recordings are remarkably alike, but they show what happened to many Cajun songs. Singers change titles and words to suit different occasions and whims. Such towns as Gueydan, Basil, Mamou, Lafayette, and Bosco are sung about and have songs named for them. "Jolie Blonde" was recorded under various titles in various places and by various real and acculturated Cajun singers. The song soon became a national hit and "Jolie Blonde's Daughter" and other relatives entered the picture. So complicated has the recording of Cajun music become, and so extensive were the recordings of Acadian songs and their adaptations and translations, that today's work in collecting and recording Cajun folk music may result in merely making copies of copies or recording songs learned from recordings.

However, a quarter of a century after Aldus Broussard made his appearance at the National Folk Festival in Dallas, he is still fiddling for dances, and his two sons, Ulysses and Austin, are carrying on, each in a separate band. All three Broussards play for several dances each week. Electrical equipment, public address systems, and amplifiers have made playing for the country dance somewhat different, but Cajun music is still Cajun music. One can identify it as far as it can be heard.

Nor were the Acadians satisfied to rest with mere singing and recordings. Dudley LeBlanc, a former state senator and the discoverer and producer of Hadacol, is supposedly the first Acadian to campaign politically by radio in French. Still another era had opened up, and Acadian music went on the air. Radio stations for many years have been broadcasting Acadian music from Crowley, Lafayette, New Iberia, Opelousas, and Abbeville. It has been possible to tune in stations from any of those towns and hear not only Acadian music and singing but also newscasts in Acadian-French, commercials and all.

JOSEPH FALCON and his family. Joe was the first Acadian accordion player and singer to record Acadian music. The late Mrs. Falcon, née Cleoma Breaux, was a singer and guitar player. Lulubelle is now a grown lady and married.

32

Cajun Mardi Gras

In the days before Lent the Acadians celebrated their traditional Mardi Gras by blending fantasy and reality for a short hilarious season when they cast aside all worries and cares. Whereas New Orleans is known the world over for a great commercialized urban Mardi Gras season, the Cajun country had a purely rural equivalent without even local newspaper publicity.

Until about 1910 many farmhouses in the cotton-and-corn section of the old Attakapas Prairie were visited annually by bands of twenty to fifty masked riders. These riders would have frightened a visitor from elsewhere clear out of his senses as they bore down at a full gallop, but not so the Acadian inhabitants. They welcomed the visits. It was a treat, a special occasion, and for them a time of celebration. The masked men were friendly neighbors, young men and boys, "running Mardi Gras" as a part of the pre-Lenten activities. They were having fun and at the same time foraging for chickens and rice and other provisions for a big Mardi Gras ball and gumbo feast. The balls were always held on the Tuesday night (just before Lent) and each owner of a *fais-dodo* had his own band of organized riders.

The owner was organizer and captain. He rode at the head of the band in civilian clothes carrying a flag as they "ran Mardi Gras" or toured in masquerade, visiting their own homes as well as those of their friends and neighbors. All procedure was according to tradition. What one group did was about the same as what the rest of them did. The announcement was made by word of mouth that the *fais-dodo* would follow its usual custom, and soon everyone was ready for the running. They generally began on Saturday morning and continued through four days. Each day they took a different road, so they covered the entire neighborhood and collected a tremendous amount of food and chickens.

Each rider, or Mardi Gras, as he was called, was dressed in a clown's suit, a high or flat hat, and a screen mask of papier mâché. The horses also received their share of decorations, which were tied to their manes, tails, and bridles. No man could run Mardi Gras unless he had a good horse, one that could stand the four days of riding. The riders often exchanged horses as a ruse. Speaking in falsetto voices furthered the deception. Part of the fun was to go to one's own house and not be recognized.

Upon approaching a farmhouse, the captain rode on ahead to ask if his band were wanted, while the band waited on the road, singing and cutting capers. If the captain dipped the flag, the band rode in at full gallop, putting all livestock to rout and sending little children scampering to their mothers. The men sang, cavorted, and played little Halloween tricks, but did no real damage. The main object was to get chickens. The men begged for and probably picked up a few eggs, but when the gift chicken was pointed out, off came their masks, and the race was on to snatch the chicken. Some farmers facetiously donated guinea fowls. Only those who have run down a guinea fowl on foot know how difficult it is to catch them, but the revelers always got their fowl—and perhaps a few more. All chickens, guinea fowls, and provisions were put in the light wagon that followed the band, and each night the load was taken to the dance hall where preparations were being made for the Mardi Gras ball and gumbo.

Imagine the feed with four big kettles of gumbo made from a hundred chickens. Everyone ate gumbo and danced until midnight, and then went home. The next morning discarded masks could be seen on all roads leading away from the *fais-dodo*, evidencing what Dickens calls "that vague kind of penitence which holidays awaken next morning." They were testimonials that the celebrations were over and that Lent had begun.

Singing was an important part of the activities while the Mardi Gras band was out on the road, even though the songs were quite elementary. Of the two songs that are best remembered, one is a drinking song and the other is a dance song. The song given here was sung by the band when they approached a house on horseback. It is characteristically Acadian in its mood, and like all songs which spring up out of the country without special composers, it uses a great deal of repetition. The Mardi Gras of this song is the masked rider or *cavalier masqué*. The first verse of the song is as follows (these verses are a fair approximation of Cajun French):

> O, Mardi Gras d'où tu viens,
> Toute 'lentour du fond du verre;
> O, Mardi Gras d'ou tu viens,
> Toute 'lentour du fond du verre;
> O, Mardi Gras d'ou tu viens,
> Toute 'lentour du fond du verre;
> Je viens de l'Angleterre,
> Oui, je viens, oui, je viens;
> Je viens de l'Angleterre,
> Oui, mon cher, oui, mon cher.

The English equivalent of that verse is:

O, Mardi Gras, from where do you come,
All around the drinking glass; [repeat three times]
I come from England,
Yes, I come, yes, I come
I come from England,
Yes, my dear, yes, my dear.

The second line evidently means "around the glass," with the superfluous words introduced to facilitate the singing. One may speculate as to why the men said they were from England. One possibility is that the only desire was to name a far-away place, and that *Angleterre* rhymed with *cher*. Another possibility is that the riders desired to convey the notion that they were bad men as perhaps Acadians thought only Englishmen could be. The words, "Yes, my dear," are used in many Acadian songs to fill in, just as the extra push-pull of the accordion is used to fill in to keep the proper time. The other verse of the song continues the story of the bottle of wine, even to the cork. This song was sung by the band as they sat waiting to find out whether or not they would be admitted to the house.

Here are the important lines of the other verse and their English equivalents:

O, Mardi Gras, quoi tu portes dans la bouteille?
Je porte du vin dans la bouteille;
La bouteille du vin est bu;
Il reste que la plein verre;
Il reste que le fond du verre;
Il reste que le rinçure;
Le rinçure du vin est bu;
Il reste que le bouchon;
Le bouchon on boira pas.

O, Mardi Gras, what have you in your bottle?
I have wine in my bottle;
The bottle of wine is drunk;
Only a glassful is left;

Only the bottom of the glass is left;
Only the rinsings are left;
The rinsings have been drunk;
Only the cork is left;
The cork, we shall not drink.

The other song most used by the Mardi Gras was the one to which they danced the *ridelle* (equivalent to our ring-around-the-rosy) and the words, as given by half a dozen men who formerly ran Mardi Gras, are these:

Là on va danser la ridelle, allons danser la ridelle;
Pour danser la ridelle on touche le pied par terre;
Pour danser la ridelle on touche le genou par terre;
Pour danser la ridelle on touche le ventre par terre;
Pour danser la ridelle on touche la tête par terre;
Pour danser la ridelle on touche le dos par terre.

The song calls for the successive touching of the foot, knee, stomach, head, and back to the ground in unison with the words. It is sung and danced after the chicken has been run down and after the masks have been removed as a final part of the visit or program. The words are as simple as words can be, and the melody is equally simple. Throughout the dance the policeman, *"paillasse,"* keeps busy with his cloth quoit in a very serious manner, flogging all erring members. After the dance the men mounted their horses and rode on to the next house with the captain leading the way, and the man with the spring wagon and chicken coop bringing up the rear.

"Running Mardi Gras" undoubtedly came out of the carnival activities of the pre-Lenten season, especially those of New Orleans. Washington, "d'Ici," jokingly called District of Courtableau and pronounced, "D. C." in St. Landry Parish, went in for an urban Mardi Gras. That town was in close touch with New Orleans through three steamboat sailings per week, and her citizens in the later decades of the last century actually put on parades with floats similar to those seen in city parades.

With the coming of the automobile, the custom of running
Mardi Gras dwindled and practically passed out, even in Lafayette, Acadia, and Evangeline parishes, where it probably was once
at its strongest. Without help from the outside, and without any
dependence upon the press, these rural people had furnished their
own entertainment and had gotten much amusement from an exciting kind of celebration of the last days before Lent.

ACADIAN MARDI GRAS. Ray Babineaux on his horse with a Mardi Gras
prize, a chicken. The masked men begged for chicken and rice, the
late Cleobule Thibodeaux followed in a wagon to carry the loot. On
Tuesday night the big celebration was held and everyone attended the
Mardi Gras ball to dance and eat chicken gumbo. (Photograph taken
in 1935.)

33

Birth, Death,
and the Social Life

THE Acadians of south-
west Louisiana are a charitable people. They have always had
that reputation, and the cases cited by Mrs. Yvonne Mouton
Whitfield bear out the statement. Mrs. Whitfield, on her father's
side, is of Acadian descent. She is thoroughly bilingual, and her
recollections of Acadian folkways and happenings from treasures
that should be recorded in complete form. Below are a few of her
recollections of occurrences, both humorous and tragic, of nearly
three-quarters of a century ago.

Because of their charitable spirit Acadians have always been willing
to help others in time of need and especially in time of sickness. Along
with this spirit of friendliness and charity went certain customs which I
believe would be of interest today.

When I was a girl, my mother and I went to the home of a neighbor
who had just lost her little baby, which was about six months old. We
arrived at the house about one o'clock, and the family had not yet had

dinner. A large group of neighbors and relatives had gathered for dinner. I, being a child at the time, did not know of their custom, so naturally I was amazed to see the great dinner that was served. They had made a table with three long planks set on sawhorses, and they had cooked chicken fricassee in a huge lard kettle. They had cooked five or six ovens of rice, all of which were soon eaten. The woman's brother who lived only half an arpent away came for dinner and brought his wife and *ten* children. This was their custom, and it was appreciated by the unfortunate and bereaved hostess. They disposed of that poor woman's entire flock of thirty chickens before it was over, but she was greatly pleased that her friends showed so much appreciation for her unfortunate circumstance. The affair showed that she had many friends; in fact, she would have been chagrined had they not come for the big meal.

Another time, Mother and I went to the home of one of our neighbors whose daughter had died of typhoid fever. We were met at the gate by one of her older daughters. The father and mother were sitting on the floor in their little two-room house, lamenting. Here, also, the neighbors and the relatives had gathered for dinner. It was January, and the day was very cold. The woman had one of her big hogs butchered to feed the guests. It was the hog she had been fattening for the year's supply of lard, but that hog was accorded the same fate as the thirty chickens of the other neighbor. That night there was not a scrap of it left.

A short time later the mother called on us to invite us to prayer meetings at her home every Sunday for nine weeks, and we were asked to attend. The following Sunday we went. Some of the poorer women had walked three or four miles to the meeting carrying their babies. The ladies formed a circle and put their babies in the center. Once in a while one of the women would have to make peace in the nursery, but this did not interfere with the prayers of the others. The hostess asked my mother to come back and bring her prayer book. These people were illiterate, and it was a novelty and a pleasure to them to hear prayers read from a book.

This woman took very good care of her children. She noticed that in the spring when she took off her baby's flannel shirt, he always caught cold. She finally worked out a plan that she thought would work to keep him from catching cold. This is the plan: "Madame Anthony, tous les jours j'ai déchiré une corde après sa chemise de flanelle; mais ça pas travaillé parce que quand j'ai ôté la dernière corde il a pris son rhume." (Every day I tore a strip off his flannel shirt. But it did not work. When I took off the last string he caught a cold.)

With one old woman lived her uncle, who was known as Vieux Misère, or "Old Misery." He was well named, for he was crippled and used a cane. He had a most sorrowful look in his face. One could not help feeling sorry for him. When it came time for Vieux Misère to depart from this life, he lingered for a few days. His wife thought that his difficulty arose from the fact that he was lying on a mattress of chicken feathers. The mattress was forthwith removed. It was one of their superstitions that chicken feathers bring bad luck and they thought that Vieux Misère would have a more peaceful death if he were not on a mattress of chicken feathers.

On this woman's farm lived a very stout woman. I never knew her real name but she was called Ma'am Bébé. Her chair and her bed were homemade. She went visiting in her only vehicle, an ox-cart. On many of her calls she refrained from getting out of her cart, as she was afraid that the floors of her friends' houses could not support her weight. She would sit all afternoon in her cart, and the friends would gather around her for the visit.

At Ma'am Bébé's house I once saw a pepper plant. I liked the sweet scented leaves, and ran to her and asked its name.

"My dear child, this is my pepper tree. That is where I get my flavoring for my food. I use the leaves in soup. I also use indigo seeds in my coffee. You see, a pound of coffee goes far with me."

She lived in a one-room house with her husband and an orphan child. One night the stout woman smothered. I went to her house on the day of the funeral. The undertaker had to take down the side of the house to remove the body.

Mrs. Whitfield's descriptions and stories of the long ago show the real warmth and generosity of the great majority of Acadian people. They have a feeling and tenderness that one can know only from personal experience.

There was also a seamier side of Acadian life which asserted itself occasionally just as it did among people of Anglo-American origin in the South who were illiterate and in otherwise unfortunate circumstances. But even among the poorest and most backward of the Acadians, there was ever present the desire on the part of the people to be accepted and to hold their heads high no matter how sad the occasion.

The following fictional sketch shows how family and neighbors gathered to pay their respects to one who had lived outside the pale of the church.

Old Basil's illness had been prolonged, and his kin and friends had scarcely expected him to pull through this time. News of his passing had traveled fast, and with it had gone the announcement of the funeral.

Old Basil had led a hard life, and he had raised a pretty hard family. He had shot a few of his neighbor's hogs he had found rooting in his potato patch, and perhaps he had left a few unpaid debts, but he had never stolen anything.

He had never been much of a man to go to church; he wasn't even a member of the church. Hence, he was not to be buried at the church cemetery but at a much smaller cemetery over at the woods. Old Azema, a neighbor woman who knew the prayers, was to do the officiating.

Long before the time set for the funeral the neighbors began to arrive in buggies, in wagons, and on horseback. Everything was in order, and Basil's remains were lying in state in the front room of his house. The men had gathered mostly on the front porch and in the front yard. They spoke in subdued voices and appeared very solemn. They talked about the weather, the crops, and different items of common gossip. They recognized each new arrival as soon as his horse came within sight at the roadside gate even though the gate was at some distance from the house.

The women, always fewer in number than the men at such occasions, congregated in the kitchen and in the backyard. Those who were kin to Basil were crying, but the others merely wore long faces. Their conversation also was in subdued tones and was mostly concerned with the deceased and the ceremony which was about to begin. Of course, they found time for a little gossip, for conversation at wakes and funerals is never confined entirely to what one might call the reason for the gathering.

Toward the middle of the afternoon old Azema began to pray.

She said the prayers long and loud, and as she did so, Basil's sons gathered about the coffin. They began to weep and mourn, and how they wept! One wondered about it, especially anyone who knew them. How tender they appeared in this hour of sorrow. Perhaps one of them remembered how many times the old man had bailed him out of jail. It may have been difficult to show such tears, but they did a good job of it.

After the prayers and the audible part of the mourning were over, the coffin was placed in a wagon, and it led the procession toward the woods. The entire procession went at a walk along the dusty road until it reached the unkempt cemetery which had only a few markers and some uncultivated cape jasmine plants scattered about in the tall grass. Basil's grave had been dug by four men who had come earlier.

More prayers were said, there was more weeping, but the interment was soon over, and the men began placing a cross over the grave. Even during the placing of the cross the weeping continued unabated until Basil's cattle brand was to be placed on the cross. Then came the first and only foul-up of the entire afternoon. The man carving the brand forgot it and sought help. Everything came to a halt until one son, under the watchful eyes of the others, carefully drew the brand with a stick in a smooth place in the dirt. This accomplished, the carving and weeping were resumed, but soon it was all over and everyone headed toward home. This time they did not travel at a walk. As one buggy hit the road, a little fellow who had felt pent up all afternoon remarked exuberantly: "Now, if we only had an accordion!"

All obligations to Basil had been fulfilled. His people were satisfied. Basil had been buried, and he had gone to his reward.

Bang! Bang! *Deux bals pour un garçon.* That was the comment that fell from the lips of those of Belizaire's neighbors who were within hearing distance of his shotgun on a still night. They had known that *La Vieille Azema,* who served as a midwife as well as a treater, had hurried over to his house as fast as old Jolivet and her cariol could take her. Now they were relieved. Belizaire had taken down his shotgun from its rack over the door, and he had gone out into the front yard and fired two shots. *Un bal pour une fille; deux bals pour un garçon.* (One shot for a girl; two shots for a boy.) It was an old Acadian custom established long before the telephone came to the prairies. The gun had told the story completely, as it had done many times before. Madame Belizaire had presented her husband with another boy.

34

An Acadian Belle
of the Nineties

IT was Marie Schexnaidre who wrote the book. She had learned to read and write while attending a convent school, and her new-found talent enabled her to record the things that to her were most important during the years just before and after her marriage which, of course, appears to have been the most important event in her life. What she did and thought, and what she had and bought were important enough to her to be recorded. Today the record helps us to reconstruct the Acadian way of life. Marie's life appears to have been quite normal, although she undoubtedly had more of the good things than most of the girls of her time and locality.

In the Nineties Marie lived on a part of what had been the old Martin Duralde vacherie in Acadia Parish, just north of Rayne. It had been a typical vacherie fronting on Bayou Plaquemine Brulée, containing both woods and prairie land. She lived at a time when the old features of Acadian life were still in vogue, but when new features were coming in. For example, she had both a spinning wheel and a sewing machine. And of course, she must have been somewhat different in that she could read and write.

Marie liked to make lists. She named the Mother Superior and the five sisters who taught her in the convent. She listed her thirty-one classmates and even the songs that they sang, such as "The Wedding Day," "The Bride's Adieu to Youth," and "The Maiden's Prayer," the words of which showed that the maiden asks for a husband with all of the virtues and no vices.

She wrote, "I attended a ball." Then she proceeded to list 122 of them, giving dates, places (by the name of owner of home or hall), and the occasion for the special dances. Most of them were week-end dances, but there were the usual holiday dances for Mardi Gras, Easter, and other such occasions. Special dances were the wedding balls which usually came in the fall of the year. For some of these she was maid of honor. Further along—"I danced with"—and she listed 187 men and boys. Apparently she named a man only when she danced with him for the first time. They were the neighborhood men and boys, many of whom were still living a decade or two ago.

On October 14, 1897, came the notice of her intention of getting married to Arthur Alleman. Then she wrote as follows:

> I was married.
> Arthur and Marie
> November 8, 1897.

Throughout the record, it was obvious that matrimony was the goal as well as the final link in the chain of social activities. But even so, Marie must have been an old maid for nearly half a dozen years, for she was twenty-two when she was married!

Dora was born on September 1, 1898; Felicia was born on July 21, 1900, and passed away on June 29, 1901; Pierre Leodice was born on April 18, 1902; and Maria was born on September 25, 1904.

The book took on a practical tone after the engagement and the wedding. From then on Marie wrote lists of purchases of clothing, furniture, utensils, little gifts for friends, and such things. Below is a list of purchases she made (with their prices)—certainly a longer list than most girls of her time could have afforded to buy. The English equivalents have been added with the help of Acadian and other friends. (The French spellings are Marie's. The author added the English equivalents.)

2	Chaise (chair)	$7.00
1	Epinglette (brooch)	.20
1	Couteau (knife)	.20
1	Voilette des portrais (portrait face veil)	$1.15
1#	Bonbon (candy)	.15
1	Colier (collar)	.10
3	Panier (basket)	.75
1	Valise (suitcase)	.70
1	Image (statue)	.10
1	Boîte (box) Baking Powder	.05
1	Fiole de limon (bottle of lemon extract)	.10
1	Moustiquaire (mosquito bar)	$1.00
8	Yarde coton (cotton cloth)	.80
1	Pot (pot)	.20
1	Plateau (platter)	.15
2	Terrine (covered dish)	.15
8	Assiette (plate)	.50
1	Berce (rocking chair)	$1.00
1	Miroir (mirror)	.25
3	Mouchoir (handkerchief)	.15
1	Ombrelle (umbrella)	.25
2	Paire Brasselet (pair of bracelets)	.20
2	Livre à corire (notebook)	.10
1	Petite Bible (testament)	.40
2	Medaille (religious medal)	$1.50
5	Images (statues)	.50
1	Medaille (religious medal)	.10
20	Yarde indienne (calico)	$1.10
5	Fiolle essence (bottle of perfume)	$1.25
	Papier et enveloppe de lettre (writing paper and envelopes)	.25

2	Poupée (doll)	.20
1	Boucle de Seinture (belt buckle)	.25
6	Culiere (spoon)	.25
2	Serviette (towel)	.40
2	Yarde coton fin (fine cotton cloth)	.10
1	Machine à coudre (sewing machine)	$16.00
1	Armoir (wardrobe)	$6.25
1	Bois de lit (bedstead)	$2.50
1	Rouet (spinning wheel)	$8.00
2	*Mouchoirs (handkerchiefs)	.50
1	Lubia (Nubia [?], head shawl)	.25
1	Epingle de cravate (tie pin)	.30
1	Baque (bucket)	$1.50
1	Paire de gant (pair of gloves)	.75
1	Cravat (tie)	.20
1	Evantaille (fan)	.50
2	Mouchoirs (handkerchiefs)	.15
1	Scapulaire (scapular)	.10
2	Yarde ruban (yard ribbon)	.15
1	Paire gant (pair of gloves)	.25
8	Yarde indienne (calico)	.40
?	Yarde coton fin (yard fine cotton cloth)	$1.25
?	Yarde coton (cotton cloth)	.80
?	Yarde gros coton (coarse cotton cloth)	.30
20#	Sucre (sugar)	$1.00
2#	Café (coffee)	.25
2	Galon de vin (gallon of wine)	.50
1#	Beur (butter)	.15
1	Fleur (flower)	.10
6	Goblet (goblet)	.25
6	Tasse (cups)	.25
6	Couteaux (knives)	.25
6	Fourchette (forks)	.25
1	Lampe (lamp)	.25
	Savon (soap)	.05
1	**Boîte poudre (box of powder)	.05

*Probably silk handkerchiefs used as mufflers.
**Probably pulverized chalk, which was used by the Acadian girls as
face powder.

2	Cadre pour encadrer des portrais (picture frames)	$1.00
1	Paire Ciseaux (pair of scissors)	.20
1	Lavabo (wash pitcher)	$1.00
1	Miroire (mirror)	.60
1	Pot et une Bol (pot and bowl)	(?)

After reading the list of things bought, one will readily see that Marie's level of living was above that of her neighbors. She bought things that other people made for themselves; she had things that the neighbors did without. With all of this she must have lived a successful life. In the words of one of her ballads, she had donned the white robe of rejoicing, and now put on the bonnet of care and the girdle of suffering. Her youthful joys were not forgotten. Their record is still treasured, while the fulfillments and the sorrows are buried with her as she sleeps in the shadow of the church which witnessed all her vows.

35

Under the Chinaberry Trees

TRAVELERS who saw the Acadian prairies before they were changed by man described with enthusiasm the rolling surface of the pure stand of waving prairie grass. With settlement, clumps of trees were planted at the farmhouses, and nearly everywhere these dotted the prairie and broke the sea of grass. These "islands" usually included any or all of three common varieties of trees: oak, catalpa, and chinaberry. Of these, the chinaberry tree was by far the most common, especially in the eastern part of the prairie, where the soil is deeper and the claypan is correspondingly farther from the surface.

For deepness of shade, no southern tree is the equal of the chinaberry or the *Lilas parasol,* as the Acadians called them. Each tree was a perfect umbrella and afforded fine shade for the people as well as for their animals. Barren indeed was the sight of the share cropper's cabin without these trees, and pitiable were his children and also his livestock unless there were trees about. The chinaberry was introduced from Asia by way of Haiti. From there it spread, although it is not especially good for wood and it is absolutely worthless for fence posts.

In spring chinaberry trees put out lilac colored flowers, hence the French name *Lilas*. Soon after the blossoms fall, seeds form as little balls or berries nearly a quarter of an inch in diameter. These the boys use as ammunition in their elderberry popguns. With the very first frost, which comes around Thanksgiving, the leaves and the berries turn a brilliant yellow which is visible, and even distinctive, for miles on a clear day. Soon the leaves and berries fall and make a great litter—but only once a year.

The berries are inedible for both man and animals but, curiously enough, robins which nest in the North and spend their winters in south Louisiana eat them and get drunk from them. While drunk they are easily caught, as they are unable to fly. They become such drunkards that the Acadians speak of people getting "as drunk as robins."

Catalpa trees, which the Acadians call *bois puant,* or stinking wood, are quite different from the chinaberry trees in that they are not as good for shade or wood, but they make excellent fence posts. The demand for catalpa fence posts caused many groves of those trees to be planted on the prairies. Still others were planted along roads and fences, where they help to beautify the landscape. Oak trees, especially live oaks, were planted about many of the houses, and in the eastern parts, water oaks grow of their own accord in limited areas, sometimes in a scattered distribution. The various oaks are to be seen in the towns and about farmhouses, wherever they have been planted and cared for.

But most interesting was the chinaberry tree in front of so many Cajun houses, where it furnished shade for the "courting horse." When a young man called on his best girl on a Sunday afternoon, he used his best horse, whether he traveled by buggy or on horseback. Of course, he tied his horse in the shade of the chinaberry tree. Anyone who passed by on the road could tell immediately who was visiting, as everyone knew all the horses of the whole neighborhood. They didn't have to ask, "Whose horse is that tied to the tree where my horse ought to be," because they knew at first sight. Not only did that horse get the play, but the family horse (the favorite courting horse in the family), a stallion, or even a race horse might spend most of the week in the shade of the chinaberry tree.

One little girl once rode a stage on the old road between Carencro and Duson. She was to get off at the house "with all of the big chinaberry trees around it." When she actually made the trip, "almost every house for the whole ten miles had chinaberry trees around it."

With the changing times, other trees are taking the place of the *Lilas parasol*. The old trees have been topped and topped so many times for firewood that their big trunks and small branches give a grotesque appearance. Windstorms have blown down many of the old trees, and others have rotted from within. It is a pity that they are decreasing in numbers, but they no longer are needed for furnishing shade for the courting horse.

CHINABERRY TREES were planted on the prairies to furnish shade and firewood. These were topped about two years previously.

36

Gri-Gri
and Monsieur le Docteur

THE old Acadians learned to take care of those who were so unfortunate as to become afflicted, whether the trouble was due to natural causes or due to a bad sign or *gri-gri* put on him by someone else. Rather than call a medical doctor, the immediate thing to do was to call a treater or *gri-gri* doctor.

Soon after 'Ti Mile was born he began to attract attention. To his parents his head seemed to be soft. They decided that he had *la tête ouverte,* or the open head. The bones were not joined together right, and something had to be done about it.

They sent for Madame Landry, the best of all of the treaters and one who was especially good for the open head. She arrived just in the nick of time. She told the parents how lucky they were that they had sent for her. She had treated many bad cases of the open head, some far worse than this one, and she had never lost a case. She had even cured cases that had been mishandled by other treaters who really did not know their business. First she always had to undo any bad work that anyone else had ever done, and then she could start in. All of this was very important.

She made a little halter of black silk and with much fanfare she placed it on 'Ti Mile's head. It was quite loose, but she said that a good treater could get results whether it was tight or not. In due time 'Ti Mile's head closed and it felt perfectly normal, all of this thanks to Madame Landry and her treatment for *la tête ouverte*. For the successful treatment she was given a little pig.

'Ti Mile's next affliction was asthma. Of course, this was not serious enough to put him to bed, but it bothered Madame Emile, so she sent for Old Girard.

Old Girard came in his cariol and began his well-known treatment. First he had 'Ti Mile stand by the gallery post and he measured him for height. Then he bored a hole in the post. Next he pulled a few hairs from 'Ti Mile's head and poked them into the hole. In a few months 'Ti Mile was tall enough to hide the hole as he stood by the post. The asthma had passed, and 'Ti Mile was a well boy, thanks to Old Girard.

Madame Belizaire's mother once developed erysipelas on the hand. She immediately called a treater, who began by making the sign of the cross, omitting the "Amen." Then he surrounded the inflammation by putting the first finger just below the elbow. Without lifting the finger he made a cross while saying, *"Au nom du Père et du Fils et du Saint-Espirit."* Then he circled his finger halfway around the arm; there he made another cross, saying, *"O, résispère je te conjure de Saint Esprit."* Then he made another cross. He kept the finger going and made another cross on the first one, so as to interlock it. Never lifting his finger from the arm until the third cross was made, he ended his treatment by making the sign of the cross in the air, omitting the "Amen." Maman soon recovered and spread the news of her cure throughout the countryside.

For other ailments the cures were not so complicated but are equally interesting. For an open wrist, such as one gets from bending corn and working too hard, one should wear a leather strap on the wrist. Treat cramps in the leg by tying a string around it. For snake bite, tie a string around the leg loosely. (Snake bites were usually on the foot or the leg.) Treat nosebleed by hanging a house key around the neck. For warts, call a treater. There are scores of *gri-gri* cures for warts, but in all probability, he will use a mud dauber nest in his treatment. For a beesting, apply a wad of well-chewed tobacco to the spot. If 'Ti Mile stepped on a rusty nail, Madame Belizaire made up a compress of raw beef and garlic, which she tied around his foot, giving the long-suffering boy an interesting aroma to carry around with him.

To cure a horse of distemper, either run him so as to "blow him out," or make him breathe smoke. Smoke him by putting some fire in the bottom of a barrel and holding his head over the barrel. For sunstroke in a horse, bleed him. This was done by using a lancet on one of the horse's neck arteries. To stop bleeding of a horse cut by barbed wire, use cobwebs and flour. The Indians also used this remedy. One cured warts on animals with mud dauber nests, just as one cured them on people. To cure blind staggers in a horse, bleed him—the same as for sunstroke.

The moon wielded a mysterious power over the land and its inhabitants. The rules are inflexible:

If you want lard, butcher your hogs on a waning moon.

If you want lean meat, butcher your hogs on a growing moon.

If you want a big crop below the ground (root crops such as potatoes, peanuts, carrots, turnips) plant in the dark of the moon.

If you want a big crop above the ground (corn, cotton, peas, beans) plant in the light of the moon.

Never look at the new moon over your left shoulder; it is *mauvaise*.

Any of the following could bring dire results:

Don't meet a corpse in the road. It will bring you bad luck.

Don't turn around in the road with a corpse when you are headed for the cemetery. It will bring bad luck.

Don't kill cats or little kittens. (That is why one sometimes sees little kittens that have been "lost" on the road.)

Don't dig in the ground on Good Friday. If you do, the ground will bleed. In fact, it is bad luck to begin any undertaking on Friday.

Don't whip a horse with a cane or a peach tree switch. If you do, it will make the horse get poor.

Don't go bare-headed in the hot sun. If you do, you will get *coup de soleil,* or sunstroke.

In order to have good luck during the new year, you must eat boiled cabbage on New Year's Day.

Don't move a broom from one house to another; it is unlucky.

Don't tell a dream before breakfast unless you want it to come true.

Despite Acadian folk medicine and "black arts," the medical profession has always been a very active one, and any doctor of established reputation had a practice that would tax the strongest and most dedicated person. Not only was the doctor overworked, but so was his horse; the individual to be most envied was the doctor's *petit nègre pour drive.* In Cajun country as throughout rural America, the country doctor needed a good horse, and a good country doctor needed two of them. When the weather and the roads were good, few people became ill. In the winter-time, when the weather and the roads were bad, he received many calls. No sooner would he return from one call than he would start out on another.

The doctor's horse had to be a big strong horse to trot right along on a muddy road. *Monsieur le docteur* had to move fast to show that he took his profession seriously. Appearances meant much. In evaluating horses even youngsters would sometimes remark: "That horse is good enough to be a doctor's horse."

To ease his own work, and perhaps to give added prestige,

some doctors used little colored boys to take care of their horses and to help with the driving. Not only did the *'ti nègre pour drive* add to his prestige, but the boy always extolled the virtues of both doctor and horse while the doctor was inside making his call. And the better the doctor and the horse were, the more important became the position of the colored boy. It was pleasant to have such fine associations, especially when all around the countryside there were the "hoodoo doctors" with their *gri-gri* treatments.

37

Cajun Country
is Festival Country

Southwest Louisiana is not without its modern festivals and celebrations. The spirit of having a good time in the Louisiana way of life fits right into the highly commercialized modern celebrations designed to draw tourists and advertise products. The center of production of each main crop or distinctive feature finds sufficient cause for holding an annual celebration based generally on the national pattern. However, communities can be distinctive.

For a complete list of festivals and pageants held in the state one should write to the Tourist Bureau, Department of Commerce and Industry, Baton Rouge, Louisiana. Here are a few notes on the festivals which are prominent in southwest Louisiana.

Although the shrimp boat harbors and home ports are marginal to the prairies, they are now within easy access. Everyone knows about the blessing of the shrimp fleet and the Louisiana

Shrimp Festival held each fall at Morgan City. Captains and crews of the many dozens, or even hundreds, of trawlers kneel aboard their craft during the invocation of the blessing. One trawler is chosen as flagship to carry priests and altar boys, and it leads the parade of gaily decorated boats up and down the Atchafalaya River. According to the program, "during the two-day celebration set to appropriate folk music, the visitors can sample the delights of the area's seafood—fish, shrimp, oysters, hard and soft shell crabs—while enjoying the festivities of this colorful atmosphere." A ride aboard a shrimp trawler in the water parade is one of the attractions offered visitors at the festival. The climax of the revelry is the shrimp fleet ball held on Sunday night. At this ball, the trawler captains and their wives and daughters make up the royal court.

Abbeville advertises a fast-growing dairy industry with a Dairy Festival which was initiated in 1949. Street dances, contests, barbecues, a queen's ball, and even a rodeo are important parts of the celebration, which draws about 100,000 people.

The International Rice Festival held each fall in Crowley advertises the area which first mechanized the production of rice and made it a commercial crop instead of the small-scale subsistence crop that it was in the old Cajun days. The twenty-fourth such festival was held on October 20-21, 1960, with three parades, two queen selections, two duck-calling contests, a frog derby, rice grading and cooking contests, a street carnival, and a livestock show. Honored guests at the 1959 festival were Mr. and Mrs. John F. Kennedy.

One of the colorful highlights of the Crowley Rice Festival is the Frog Derby which is sponsored by the Lions Club of the nearby town of Rayne. That town, for more than half a century, has been known as the Frog Capital of the World. The competition in frog jumping leads to selection of a champion, but perhaps more important, the selection of "frog jockies," from whom a queen is selected. Winners usually make the trip to Calaveras,

California, for the international frog-jumping championship in
the town which Mark Twain made famous in his story "The
Jumping Frog of Calaveras."

Lafayette has long been famous for flowers. Camellias are
found in abundance and are featured in the annual Camellia
Pageant. Lafayette is also a favorite point of interest along the
beautiful Azalea Trail. Joel L. Fletcher, president of the University of Southwestern Louisiana, decided in 1935 to honor the camellia in an annual pageant. He initiated the Camellia Pageant
which became an added attraction to the South Louisiana Mid-
Winter Fair which he had inaugurated in 1927 while he was dean
of agriculture at the Lafayette institution. H. K. Riley, professor
of horticulture, for many years had charge of the planning of the
pageant, and faculty and students alike, through their different
departments, have co-operated to make the Camellia Pageant a
beautiful attraction of national significance.

Instead of having a jubilee celebration, Opelousas holds a "Yambilee" to honor a potato king and queen, and incidentally to advertise yams and sweet potatoes. It should be noted here that the
area around Opelousas is the center of the heaviest sweet potato
production in the country.

New Iberia holds a Sugar Cane Festival. The banks of Bayou
Têche, on which that town is located, have been famous for sugar
production for more than a century and a half, and it is befitting
that the city should honor the crop that is still its main support.

St. Martinville, in 1955, held a special celebration, the occasion
being the 200th anniversary of the expulsion of the Acadians from
Nova Scotia by the British. Through much of that year various
activities depicting Acadian history and culture were scheduled.
All of them helped to stimulate interest and activity on the part
of the inhabitants, and they also served as an attraction to tourists.

38

Revolution
in the Beef Cattle Industry

THE development of the beef cattle industry in southwest Louisiana, as in the entire South, is only a part of a great and fast-changing economic structure. Actually, it is a part of the agricultural revolution. When one sees how much has been learned and what has been done in the past few decades, and the importance of it all, one wonders why the improvements did not come sooner. "What My Father Didn't Know About Raising Beef Cattle" probably is the most important paper that a Cajun cattleman could write today. The past generation was held back by a great variety of factors, and beef cattle raising was no exception. A vicious circle of adverse conditions impeded, retarded, and even stymied the cattle man.

A farmer couldn't bring in good cattle because they didn't do well on the poor feed. Even if they survived the tick fever, there still were flies, mosquitoes, and other pests for them to contend with. The good grasses had not yet been introduced or developed, and most of them would not have done well without heavy application of fertilizer and improved practices in their handling. With those handicaps and with cotton, sugar cane, and other commercial crops being the centers of attention, it is no wonder that scrub cattle were so numerous and stood the better chances for survival.

Fortunately, the vicious cycle has been broken. More and better beef is being produced all of the time because of:

1.   Improvement in the cattle themselves through introduction of better breeds, by upgrading, and through crossbreeding.

2.   Improvement in feed, especially in the use of better grasses on improved soil conditions, and better grazing practices.

3.   Better care of the cattle, especially in protecting them from pests and diseases which formerly prevented the introduction of animals of quality and retarded the growth of the inferior animals that were kept.

New developments have come about largely through the work of agriculture departments on the national, state, and parish levels. Universities and agricultural colleges, experiment stations and extension services, high schools, through their agriculture courses and 4-H and FFA clubs, cattlemen's and breeders' associations, fairs and shows, fertilizer and insecticide industries, newspapers and other periodicals, and radio and television stations have all been more than willing to help the farmer with his grassland farming and cattle problems.

Breeds and breeding of cattle. The story of the old cattle industry in southwest Louisiana has been told earlier where it was stated that longhorns and various types of scrub cattle were the cattle of the Cajun prairies. Nowadays, as one drives through Cajun country, one sees at every hand evidence of the introduction of better stock. The modern breeds introduced are mainly Herefords, Aberdeen Angus, and Shorthorn, but a few of the other European breeds, such as the Charollaise, are represented.

Then, of course, the dairy breeds are well represented in Jerseys and Holsteins. While these are kept for dairy purposes, every dairy cow is a potential beef animal, and many of the butcher calves that are marketed have dairy blood in them.

Brahman cattle now play an important part in the cattle industry in south Louisiana.[1] The story of their introduction has been told many times, but it might be stated here that they were introduced into the South more than a century ago. They were on their way toward successful development when the Civil War and one condition after another caused them to be killed off, absorbed, and lost. Introductions in the early part of this century were successful, but the animals brought in, although perhaps the best in India, were not up to the standards of good European cattle. Much credit is due the breeders of these cattle for improving them to the high standards found in the better herds along the Gulf Coast.

Their main virtue lay in their hardiness, a trait which had come through thousands of years of development in hot country, where they received little care and where ideals and standards were quite different from our own. Probably the main selection that went on was determined by ability to survive periods of famine. This was the picture of Brahman cattle in the South when the animal breeder and geneticist entered the scene.

Through selective breeding and better feeding and care, Brahman cattle have. been greatly improved. Most of them now are mild mannered, and generally they are handled the way European cattle are handled. Although at times they are difficult to drive or crowd, they are easily led, and can be trained to follow when called. In conformation, the best Brahmans are beginning to approach European cattle. When it is recalled that the up-breeding has gone on for only forty or fifty years, the improvement is astounding. But it is for crossbreeding that Brahmans are most val-

[1]See William Stats Jacobs, "History of Brahman Importations," *The American Brahman* (October, 1955), 8-11; Harry P. Gayden, "The Louisiana Brahman Industry Began in 1854," *Gulf Coast Cattleman* (February, 1952), 29-32.

uable. They and European cattle cross readily, and not only are
their offspring fertile, but they show the fleshing qualities of European cattle and the hardiness of the Brahmans *plus* a hybrid vigor
or heterosis of their own.

Unfortunately, much of the crossing has been of a haphazard
nature. One may see in herds of cattle along the Gulf Coast region
traits of the Brahman, Hereford, Aberdeen Angus, and several
of the dairy breeds of European cattle mixed into almost any and
all combinations. But the systematic breeders have been at work
with scientific breeding and principles of genetics. At experiment
stations and in agriculture departments of colleges, as well as in
private enterprise, the work has gone on for decades. Yet even the
scientists are still divided as to what might be the real objective
in crossing breeds. Here are two very different plans, each of which
has its followers.

One plan is to cross two pure breeds with the hope of finding
just which crosses produce hybrid vigor and carry over the best
qualities of both parents. The other plan aims to produce, fix, and
maintain new breeds with all of the good features of two or even
three original breeds and also to retain the prepotency of the hybrid vigor for generation after generation without deterioration.[2]
Santa Gertrudis cattle developed in Texas have all the necessary
qualifications of a new breed, and they fall in this latter category.
They have made their appearance in southwest Louisiana and will
have an opportunity to show their worth.[3]

From the preceding, one might infer that little remains to be
done in the improvement of cattle in Cajun country or in the
South. Such is not the case. One of the greatest needs in the cattle
industry today is improvement of the stock. However, cattlemen
are active along this line, and any one who has seen the changes of

[2]See S. L. Crochet, "More Beef From Crossbreds," *Breeders' Gazette* (July, 1958),
8-9; A. L. Baker and W. H. Black, "Crossbred Types of Beef Cattle for the Gulf
Coast Region," *The American Brahman* (May, 1954), 29, 66.

[3]See Robert J. Klegberg, Jr., *The Santa Gertrudis Breed of Cattle* (pamphlet published by the King Ranch, n.d.).

the past quarter-century would agree that a fine start has been made in the improvement of beef stock.

Better grass. The grasses of the prairies were not naturally good grasses. They were much less nourishing than the grasses of the semiarid West. Carpetgrass, which took over at an early time, still is not a very good grass. The meagerness of the grazing was held down by the attention that farmers paid to "row crops." Grass was not a crop; it was a pest in the cleanly tilled fields. Poor grass from poor soil made poor cattle. With the coming of some of the so-called pests, such as Bermuda grass and Johnson grass, there was some improvement in feed. Still other grasses, such as Dallis grass, are being tried, but they are not of widespread distribution or use. Shortage of good winter grazing is undoubtedly the area's greatest drawback. Rye grass, fescue, clovers, and other grazing crops are getting some attention.[4]

Of special local interest on the natural prairies in southwest Louisiana is a type of agricultural enterprise which is productive of beef and rice. Since rice could not be planted year after year on the same land, there developed a system of alternating between planting rice and allowing cattle to graze off the unwanted volunteer red rice and any other grass which might grow during the off year. This system is now outmoded, and scientific experimentation and practices have shown that both rice and cattle production can be greatly increased through better planned systems of rotation. One plan calls for a four-year rotation system with two years in rice followed by two in improved pasture. Another plan calls for a six-year rotation with two rice crops followed by four years of pasturing. Probably the main benefit derived from the new plans lies in the planting of such improved forage crops as Lespedeza, Dallis grass, and Dutch clover, but another reason for the success of the grasses and clovers in producing beef is that nowadays the rice farmers go in heavily for fertilizing. Thus the

---

[4]See Glenn W. Burton, "Grassland Improvement: A Vast Potential," *Journal of Agricultural and Food Chemistry*, III, No. 1 (January, 1955), 23-31.

fertilizers, the improved grasses and clovers, the better breeds of
cattle give many times the quantity of beef that was produced
under the old system, and the land is left in such good condition
that the rice crop during the succeeding two years is greatly increased. The whole plan fits into the general agricultural revolution which is going on in the South and, no doubt, will continue
to change and improve with future scientific development.[5]

Better care of cattle. With better cattle and better grass, it follows that the cattle themselves need better care, and they are getting it. The water problem is not great, and the shade problem
is partially solved.

The chemical industries should be mentioned for one of the
great contributions to the cattle industry—insecticides and other
means of fighting pests. These include not only dusts and sprays,
but also solutions for dipping vats. The dipping vat came into use
in the opening of the fight against ticks and tick fever, but it is
also used to some extent in the battle against other ticks, flies,
mosquitoes, lice, and whatever other insects bite cattle.

As the cattleman must ever be alert to see that open cuts and
scratches do not get infected, especially in fly time, he uses smears,
sprays, and dusts whenever he earmarks, brands, dehorns, or cas-
trates animals.

Nor does he stop with the external treatments and preventa-
tives. Vaccines save cattle from anthrax, blackleg, and other diseases. The cattleman treats his cattle internally for liver flukes
and other parasites that might kill his stock, or at least retard their
growth. If he doesn't employ the services of a veterinarian, he has
to be quite a scientist in order to handle safely and efficiently all
of the treatments necessary to insure the protection of his herd.

Altogether, cattle today get far better treatment than they received formerly. There is no comparison between the old "cow

[5]See Post, "The Rice Country of Southwest Louisiana," *The Geographical Review,* XXX, No. 4 (October, 1940), 574-90; Fred Hurst, "Louisiana's New Pasture-
Rice Rotation," *The Progressive Farmer* (April, 1951), 16, 122; Charles W. Price, Jr.,
"Less Work, More Rice, More Beef," *The Progressive Farmer* (September, 1948), 17,
101.

hunting" days, when they were chased on horseback and with dogs, and the way they are hauled in trucks today. Due to the careful planning of the pastures, lanes, gates, and chutes, it is possible to handle cattle on many farms without the use of horses, and the lariat is rather generally outmoded. The progressive cattleman pays particular attention to preventing his cattle from losing weight. That is something that *any* farmer can understand, especially since cattle are sold by weight.

While numbers of cattle have been decreasing in the arid Southwest, they have been increasing in the humid South. Of that increase, southwest Louisiana has had its full share. Not only have cattle increased in numbers, but their quality probably has made an even greater gain.[6]

---

[6]See Dave L. Pearce, "Louisiana Building for the Future of the Cattle Industry," *Gulf Coast Cattleman* (February, 1953), 7-8, 10; Troy H. Middleton, "LSU and the Cattle Industry," *Gulf Coast Cattleman* (May, 1951), 17-19; A. P. Parham, "The Cattle Industry in Louisiana," *Livestock Magazine* (September, 1957), 4, 30-31.

39

Cajuns Today

TODAY there is growing pride in Acadian ancestry. Any Acadian is related to or knows others who have made good and have been a credit to their ancestry. Nor have their successful activities been confined to the local area. Their men have served with distinction in both world wars, and the experiences and travels have broadened them, so that they make more useful citizens when they come home. Acadians do considerable traveling in this country; some go to French Canada to see the land of their forefathers; still others have taken educational and religious tours in Europe.

Cajuns participate in sports and many kinds of competition in which they acquit themselves admirably. In high school, those who are interested in agriculture may receive the benefits of experience in 4-H and FFA work. Their training may continue while they are in college where they gain valuable experience in stock judging and all phases of scientific agriculture.

Education is a great equalizer. Many Acadians attend such colleges as University of Southwestern Louisiana at Lafayette, McNeese State College in Lake Charles, and Louisiana State University in Baton Rouge.

Back in the thirties there was a strong trend away from Cajun music. The accordion was old fashioned, and the young people fell in line with the modern styles of music. But there has been a reversal, and Cajun music has had a strong representation in recordings and broadcasts over the air. In similar fashion Cajun French has been used in newscasts and radio commercials. It is just as convenient to listen to the news in French, and it is a lot more fun. Listeners developed the habit of following their favorite newscasters, who are bilingual, to such an extent that they can read and translate the news into Cajun French right out of the morning newspaper.

In the Acadian homes of today the equipment and appliances are not inferior to those of rural America in general. Enter the home of a farmer who would be expected to be living in very modest circumstances, and you might expect to find a meagerly furnished dwelling. Such would not be the case, for rural electrification has reached practically all homes. Electric refrigerators, freezers, fans, washing machines, irons, toasters, and other equipment are commonplace. If natural gas is not available, the butane tank almost invariably is. The radio is universal, and even on old Cajun houses one sees the ubiquitous television aerial.

The cotton farmer makes an effort to get instruction in the use of commercial fertilizers and insecticides in order to get maximum production on his limited cotton allotment. By doing so he can get several times the yield that his grandfather got on the same land. He knows about hybrid seed corn, and he plants the best seed that he can get.

He has no excuse for not getting the best in breeds of chickens, hogs, or cattle. If he is a dairyman he can use the services of the artificial insemination station at Louisiana State University. He knows about and has seen some of the best purebred stock in the whole country.

In every phase of life the modern and the scientific are available. They may be used. If not, it probably is because there are some pleasant features in the old. Let us hope that with the modern change many of the old features will remain. This book records just a portion of the old. Let us hope that the rest is recorded soon, for when it is all replaced, we can truthfully say that an important and pleasant part of the American way of life will have been lost.

Bibliography

MANUSCRIPTS

"Baptismal Records," 1765 to present. Catholic Church, St. Martinville.

"Brand Book for the Districts of Opelousas and Attakapas, 1760–1880." Handwritten copy presented to the Stephens Memorial Library, University of Southwestern Louisiana, by Mrs. Gradney Cochran.

"Census Data Schedules, United States Census for Louisiana, 1810–1860." Archives of Duke University Library, Durham, North Carolina.

"Census for the Parish of St. Landry in the State of Louisiana, November 1, 1858." Lists the qualified voters; number of white people by families; number of slaves of each head of household; number of free Negroes by households, their slaves; male whites eighteen to forty-five years of age. Lists 12,236 slaves; 1,596 free Negroes; and a total population of 25,801.

SAMUEL HENRY LOCKETT. "Louisiana As It Is: A Geographical and Topographical Description of the State. . . ." 1873. Original copy in the Tulane University Library. Edited copies in the writer's possession and in the library of the Louisiana State University.

"Marie Schixnaidre's Diaries, Reminiscences, and Accounts," telling of experiences and expenditures from 1892–1904. Written in French in a very elementary but sincere style, it gives insight into life of French-speaking family near Bayou Wikoff about two miles north of Rayne in Acadia Parish. Book in possession of her son, Leodice Alleman of Rayne in 1935.

"Reminiscences of Thomas C. Nichols, 1840." The author of this manuscript was the son of a *Grand Juge* (judge) in Attakapas during the years immediately following the Louisiana Purchase. He recalls experiences from about 1805, tells of life in New Orleans, the trip to Attakapas by boat, and life in the Attakapas Country. Copy in possession of Mrs. Mary Flower Pugh Russell, grand-daughter of Mr. Nichols.

"Spanish Surveys of Louisiana, Books E–J" (about 10 volumes), various dates. Contain plats and descriptions of individual grants. Library, Louisiana State University, Baton Rouge.

BOOKS

ALLIOT, PAUL. *Historical and Political Reflections of Louisiana.* Lorient, France, 1803. Trans. and reprinted in J. A. Robertson, ed., *Louisiana Under the Rule of Spain, France, and the United States, 1785–1807,* I, 29–143.

American State Papers: Documents, Legislative and Executive, of the Congress of the United States, Public Lands. 8 vols. Washington, 1832–1861.

ARNOLD, OREN AND HALE, JOHN P. *Hot Irons.* New York, 1944.

ARTHUR, STANLEY C. *The Fur Bearing Animals of Louisiana.* (Department of Conservation, Bulletin No. 18.) New Orleans, 1928.

BARDE, ALEXANDRE. *Historic des Comités de Vigilance aux Attakapas.* St. Jean Baptiste, Louisiana, 1861.

BOLTON, HEBERT E. (ed.). *Athanese de Mézières and the Louisiana-Texas Frontier, 1768–1780.* 2 vols. Cleveland: The Arthur H. Clark Co., 1914.

BOUCHEREAU, L. *Statement of the Sugar and Rice Crops Made in Louisiana in 1870–1871 With an Appendix.* New Orleans, 1871.

BRACKENRIDGE, HENRY M. *Views of Louisiana; Together with a Journal of a Voyage up the Missouri River in 1811.* Pittsburgh, 1814.

BROUSSARD, JAMES. *Louisiana Creole Dialect.* Baton Rouge: Louisiana State University Press, 1942.

CABLE, GEORGE W. *Bonaventure: A Prose Pastoral of Acadian Louisiana.* New York, 1888.

CHAMBERS, HENRY E. *A History of Louisiana.* Chicago: The American Historical Society, 1925.

CHOPIN, KATE. *Bayou Folk.* Boston and New York, 1894.

CHOPIN, KATE. *A Night in Acadie.* 2nd ed. Chicago, 1897

DARBY, WILLIAM. *A Geographical Description of the State of Louisiana.* New York, 1817.

DAVIS, EDWIN ADAMS. *Louisiana: The Pelican State.* Baton Rouge: Louisiana State University Press, 1959.

DEILER, J. HANNO. *The Settlement of the German Coast of Louisiana.* Philadelphia: American Germanica Press, 1909.

DENHARDT, ROBERT M. *The Horse of the Americas.* Norman: University of Oklahoma Press, 1948.

DENNETT, DANIEL. *Louisiana As It Is—Its Topography and Material Resources. . . .* New Orleans, 1876.

DIMITRY, JOHN. *History and Geography of Louisiana.* New Orleans, 1877.

DITCHY, JAY KARL. *Les Acadiens Louisianais et Leur Parler.* Baltimore: The Johns Hopkins University Press, 1932.

DOUGHTY, ARTHUR G. *The Acadian Exiles: A Chronicle of the Land of Evangeline.* Toronto, 1916.

EWING, JASPER G. *Louisiana: A Tourist Guide to Points of General Interest.* Baton Rouge: n.p., 1932.

FLETCHER, JOEL L. *The Louisiana Acadians Today, An Address Delivered to Cambridge Historical Society.* Lafayette: University of Southwestern Louisiana, 1948.

FORTIER, ALCÉE. *A History of Louisiana.* 4 vols. New York: Goupil and Co., 1904.

FORTIER, ALCÉE. *Louisiana Studies.* New Orleans, 1894.

FRENCH, BENJAMIN. *Historical Collections of Louisiana.* 5 vols. New York, 1846–76.

GAYARRE, CHARLES. *History of Louisiana.* 4 vols. New Orleans: F. F. Hansell and Bros., 1903.

GRIFFIN, HARRY L. *The Attakapas Trail.* Lafayette: n.p., 1923.

HARRIS, WILLIAM H. *Louisiana Products, Resources and Attractions With a Sketch of the Prairies.* New Orleans, 1881.

HILGARD, EUGENE W. "Physico-geographical and Agricultural Features of the State of Louisiana. *(10th Census of the United States)* Washington, 1884.

HOWE, HENRY V., and MORESI, CYRIL K. *Geology of Lafayette and St. Martin Parishes* ("Geological Bulletin No. 3.") Baton Rouge: Louisiana Department of Conservation, 1933.

JEFFERSON, JOSEPH. *The Autobiography of Joseph Jefferson.* New York, 1889.

JOHNSTON, MARGARET A. (ed.). *In Acadia: The Acadians in Story and Song.* New Orleans, 1893.

KAMMER, EDWARD J. *A Socio-Economic Survey of the Marshdwellers of Four Southeastern Louisiana Parishes.* ("The Catholic University of America Studies in Sociology," Vol. 3.) Washington, 1941.

KANE, HARNETT T. *Plantation Parade: The Grand Manner in Louisiana.* New York: W. Morrow and Co., 1945.

KANE, HARNETT T. *The Bayous of Louisiana.* New York: W. Morrow and Co., 1943.

KING, GRACE. *Creole Families of Louisiana.* New York, 1921.

KNAPP, SEAMAN. *Rice Culture.* ("United States Department of Agriculture Farmers' Bulletin," No. 417) Washington, 1910.

LABAT, JEAN BAPTISTE. *Nouveau Voyage aux Iles de l'Amérique.* 2d ed. 2 vols. Paris, 1724.

LEBLANC, DUDLEY J. *The True Story of the Acadians.* Lafayette: n.p., 1932.

LE PAGE DU PRATZ, ANTOINE S. *Histoire de la Louisiane.* 3 vols. Paris, 1758.

Louisiana: A Guide to the State. ("American Guide Series.") New York: Hastings House, 1941.

Louisiana Rice Book. Lake Charles, La.: Passengers Department of Southern Pacific Railroad Company, 1900.

MCVOY, LIZZIE CARTER. *A Bibliography of Fiction by Louisianians and on Louisiana Subjects.* Baton Rouge: Louisiana State University Press, 1935.

MARTIN, FRANÇOIS-XAVIER. *The History of Louisiana.* Rev. ed. New Orleans, 1882.

MEYER, A. H. and HENRICKSON, B. H. *Soil Survey of Lafayette Parish.* ("United States Department of Agriculture Bulletin") Washington, 1919.

OLMSTED, FREDERICK LAW. *A Journey in the Seaboard Slave States.* New York, 1856.

PERRIN, WILLIAM H. (ed.). *Southwest Louisiana, Biographical and Historical.* New Orleans, 1891.

RAMSEY, CAROLYN. *Cajuns on the Bayous.* New York: Hastings House, 1957.

READ, WILLIAM A. *Louisiana-French.* Baton Rouge: Louisiana State University Press, 1931.

ROBERTSON, JAMES ALEXANDER. *Louisiana Under the Rule of Spain, France and the United States, 1785-1807.* Cleveland: The Arthur H. Clark Co., 1911.

ROBIN, C. C. *Voyages dans l'Intérieur de la Louisiane, de la Floride Occidentale et dans les Isles de la Martinique et de St.-Domingue Pendent les Années 1802, 1804, 1805, et 1806.* 3 vols. Paris, 1807.

ROWLAND, DUNBAR *(ed). Official Letter Books of W. C. C. Claiborne, 1801–1816.* 6 vols. Jackson: State Department of Archives and History, 917.

ST. MARTIN, THADDEUS. *Madame Toussaint's Wedding Day.* Boston: Little, Brown and Co., 1936.

SAVILLE, R. J. *Factors in the Successful Operation of Louisiana Rice Farms, 1930.* ("Louisiana State University Bulletin 233") Baton Rouge, 1933.

SAUCIER, CORINNE L. *Folk Tales From French Louisiana.* New York, 1962.

SAXON, LYLE (comp.). *Gumbo Ya-Ya.* Boston: Houghton Mifflin Co., 1945.

SCROGGS, WILLIAM O. *The Story of Louisiana.* Indianapolis, 1924.

SEALSFIELD, CHARLES. *The Cabin Book of Sketches of Life in the Southwest.* New York, 1844.

SEGURA, PEARL MARY. *The Acadians in Fact and Fiction: A Classified Bibliography of Writing on the Subject of Acadians in the Stephens Memorial Library, SLI.* Baton Rouge: Department of Commerce, 1955.

SMITH, T. LYNN, and HITT, HOMER L. *The People of Louisiana.* Baton Rouge: Louisiana State University Press, 1952.

STODDARD, AMOS. *Sketches Historical and Descriptive of Louisiana.* Philadelphia, 1812.

STUBBS, W C. *Sugar Cane: A Treatise in the History, Botany, and Agriculture of Sugar Cane.* Louisiana Bureau of Agriculture, 1897.

VINCENT, JOSEPH J. *Streak O'Lean and a Streak O'Fat.* Ed. Southern Historical Associates, Publishers. Tampa, Florida, 1953.

VOORHIES, FELIX. *Acadian Reminiscences, With the True Story of Evangeline.* Opelousas: The Jacobs News Co., 1911.

WARD, NOAH. *Official Brand Book of the State of Louisiana. . . .* 2nd ed. Baton Rouge: The Department of Agriculture and Immigration, Livestock Brand Commission, 1955.

WHITFIELD, IRÈNE THÉRESÈ. *Louisiana French Folk Songs.* Baton Rouge: Louisiana State University Press, 1939.

WINZERLING, OSCAR WILLIAM. *Acadian Odyssey.* Baton Rouge: Louisiana State University Press, 1955.

ARTICLES

BARBEAU, MARIUS. "Louisiana French," *Canadian Geographical Journal,* LIV, No. 1 (January, 1957), 2-11.

CARPENTER, W. M. "Miscellaneous Notices in Opelousas and Attakapas," *American Journal of Science,* XXXV (1839), 344-46.

COSTA, FERNANDO SOLANO. "The Acadian Migration to Spanish Louisiana," trans. by G. B. ROBERTS. *Southwestern Louisiana Journal* (Winter, 1958), 2-44.

CROWLEY *Signal,* Magazine Section No. 2 of the *Signal* Annual, December 19, 1908.

CROWLEY *Signal,* Prosperity Number, May, 1898.

CROWLEY *Signal,* Rice Number, January 30, 1904.

DANIELS, R. L. "The Acadians of Louisiana," *Scribner's Monthly,* XIX (1880), 383-92.

DART, HENRY P., "Slavery in Louisiana," *Louisiana Historical Quarterly,* VII, No. 2 (April, 1924), 332-33.

DITCHY, JAY K. (trans.). "Early Census Tables of Louisiana," *Louisiana Historical Quarterly,* XIII, No. 2 (April, 1930), 205-29.

FLOWERS, FRANK C. "Longfellow in Louisiana on His One Hundred Fiftieth Anniversary," *Southwestern Louisiana Journal* (Winter, 1958), 45-49.

FORTIER, ALCÉE. "The Acadians and Their Dialect," *Publications of the Modern Language Association of America,* VI, No. 1 (1891), 1-33.

GAYDEN, HARRY P. "The Louisiana Brahman Cattle Industry Began in 1854," *Gulf Coast Cattleman* (February, 1952), 29-32.

GAYNOR, W. C. "Acadia and Acadians," *Magazine of History*, XVI (June, 1913), 221-35.

GINN, MILDRED KELLY. "A History of Rice Production in Louisiana to 1896," *Louisiana Historical Quarterly*, XXIII, No. 2 (April, 1940), 544-88.

JOHNSON, E. D. "A Brief Historiography of Louisiana," *Southwestern Louisiana Journal*, II (Spring, 1958), 107-25.

KELLY, MINNIE. "Acadian South Louisiana," *Journal of Geography*, XXXIII, No. 3 (March, 1934), 81-90.

KNAPP, EDWIN. "Southwest Louisiana's Thriving Cattle Industry," *Gulf Coast Cattleman* (October, 1952), 9-10.

KNIFFEN, FRED B. "Louisiana House Types," *Annals of the Association of American Geographers*, XXVI, No. 4 (December, 1935), 179-93.

MIDDLETON, TROY H. "LSU and the Cattle Industry," *Gulf Coast Cattleman* (May, 1951), 17-19.

MOODY, VERNIE ALTON. "Slavery on the Louisiana Plantations," *Louisiana Historical Quarterly*, VII (1924), 191-301.

OSTER, HARRY. "Acculturation in Cajun Folk Music," *The McNeese Review*, X (Winter, 1959), 12-24.

PARENTON, VERNON J. "Notes on the Social Organization of a French Village in South Louisiana," *Social Forces*, XVII (October, 1938), 73-82.

PARHAM, A. P. "The Cattle Industry in Louisiana," *Livestock Magazine* (September, 1957), 4, 30-31.

PORTEOUS, LAURA L. "Inventory of de Vaugine's Plantation in the Attakapas on Bayou Têche, 1773," *Louisiana Historical Quarterly*, IX, No. 4 (October, 1926), 570-89.

POST, LAUREN C. "Acadian Animal Caste in Southwest Louisiana: Some Sociological Observations," *Rural Sociology*, V, No. 2 (June, 1940), 183-91.

POST, LAUREN C. "An Acadian Art: Hand Weaving in the Attakapas Country of Southwestern Louisiana," *Louisiana State University Alumni News*, XI, No. 3 (March, 1935), 18-19, 36.

POST, LAUREN C. "Acadian Contracts in Southwest Louisiana: Some Sociological Observations," *Rural Sociology*, VI, No. 2 (June, 1941), 144-55.

POST, LAUREN C. "Acadian Folkways," *Louisiana State University Alumni News*, XII, No. 4 (April, 1936), 6-9, 26-27.

POST, LAUREN C. "Acadian Mardi Gras," *Louisiana State University Alumni News*, XII, No. 1 (January, 1936), 8-10, 31-32.

POST, LAUREN C. "Cattle Branding in Southwest Louisiana," *The McNeese Review*, X (Winter, 1958), 101-17.

POST, LAUREN C. "The Domestic Animals and Plants of French Louisiana as Mentioned in the Literature With Reference to Sources, Varieties, and Uses," *Louisiana Historical Quarterly*, XVI (October, 1933), 544-86.

POST, LAUREN C. "The Landscape in its Annual Cycle on the Prairies of Southwest Louisiana," *Journal of Geography*, XXXVIII, No. 7 (October, 1939), 267-75.

POST, LAUREN C. "The Old Cattle Industry of Southwest Louisiana," *The McNeese Review*, IX (Winter, 1957), 43-55.

POST, LAUREN C. "Revolution of the Beef Cattle Industry in the South," *The McNeese Review*, XI (Winter, 1959), 61-75.

POST LAUREN C. "The Rice Country of Southwestern Louisiana," *The Geographical Review*, XXX, No. 4 (October, 1940), 574-90

RUSSELL, RICHARD J. "Flotant," *Geographical Review*, XXXII, No. 1 (January, 1942), 74-98.

RUSSELL, RICHARD J. and HOWE, HENRY V. "Cheniers of Southwestern Louisiana," *The Geographical Review*, XXV, No. 3 (July, 1935), 449-61.

SANDOZ, W. J. "A Brief History of St. Landry Parish," *Louisiana Historical Quarterly*, VIII (April, 1925), 221-39.

SCROGGS, WILLIAM O. "Rural Life in the Lower Mississippi Valley," *Proceedings Mississippi Valley Historical Association*, VIII (1914-1915).

SEGURA, PEARL MARY. "A Bibliography of Acadiana," *Southwestern Louisiana Journal*, II (Spring, 1958), 170-212. Lists titles in the University of Southwestern Louisiana library only.

SMITH, T. LYNN, and PARENTON, VERNON J. "Acculturation Among the Louisiana French," *American Journal of Sociology*, XLIV (November, 1938), 355-64.

SMITH, T. LYNN and POST, LAUREN C. "The Country Butchery: A Co-operative Institution," *Rural Sociology*, II, No. 3 (September, 1937), 335-37.

STEPHENS, EDWIN L. "The Story of Acadian Education in Louisiana," *Louisiana Historical Quarterly*, XVIII, No. 2 (July, 1935), 397-406.

SUGAR, LEON. "Following the Spanish Trail Across the 'Neutral Territory' in Louisiana," *Louisiana Historical Quarterly*, X, No 1 (January, 1927), 86-93.

SURFACE, GEORGE THOMAS. "Rice in the United States," *Geographic Society Bulletin*, XLIII (July, 1911), 500-509

WARNER, DUDLEY. "The Acadian Land," *Harper's Magazine* (February 18, 1887), 334-54.

Index

Leissez les bons temps rouler

11/05.